WRITE YOUR SELF

*A comprehensive guide to using writing techniques
for developing a new understanding of yourself*

Stephen Wade

First published in 2017
© Copyright 2017
Stephen Wade

The right of Stephen Wade to be identified as the author of this work has been asserted by her in accordance with Copyright, Designs and Patents Act 1998.

All rights reserved. No reproduction, copy or transmission of this publication may be made without written permission. No paragraph of this publication may be reproduced, copied or transmitted save with the written permission or in accordance with the provisions of the Copyright Act 1956 (as amended).

Any person who does any unauthorised act in relation to this publication may be liable to criminal prosecution and civil claims for damage.

Although every effort has been made to ensure the accuracy of the information contained in this guide as of the date of publication, nothing herein should be construed as giving specific treatment advice. This publication is intended to provide general information pertaining to developing these skills.

ISBN Paperback 978-1-78705-192-8
ISBN ePub 978-1-78705-193-5
ISBN PDF 978-1-78705-194-2

Published in the UK by MX Publishing, 335, Princess Park Manor, Royal Drive, London, N11 3GX
www.mxpublishing.co.uk

Cover design by Brian Belanger

Contents

List of illustrations
Introduction

1. Taking stock of the raw data
Seeing your present creative potential
Shaking off failure
Asking positive questions
Educating yourself emotionally
Being a child, seeing as a child
Case study
Summary

2. Making other selves from your present self
Journaling for self-insights
Writing about your journey so far
Writing about now
Being a poet of your 'little universe'
Writing dialogues
Case Study
Summary

3. Escaping the catharsis trap
Knowing your feelings honestly
Learning *narratories*
Writing narratories about fears
What the Greeks thought – cleansing things
Creating different points of view
Case study
Summary

4. Writing for well-being
Words –giving therapy
Ideas- knowing the sanity of your imaginings
Compiling a personal anthology
Learning from patience/patients
Listening to other's sub-texts

Case study
Summary

5. Life-scripts and adapting endings
Not writing that obituary
Writing from the affirmatives
Making the little universe spin
What and why you love
Spinning epics of success
Case study
Summary

6. The docudrama of your present
Looking from the outside in
Your creative p.o.v. explained
Handling the camerawork
Bringing in the creative scriptwriter
Researching the audience of one
Case study
Summary

7. Sharpening skills of self-development
Introducing workshops
Doing the Workshop of One routine
Planning your workshops
Sharing your workshops
Checking on the skills so far
Case study
Summary

8. Life-writing
Introducing the new autobiographies
Some masters explained
How we learn from writers
Patterning life-writing
Using a classic: Plato's cave
Case study
Summary

9. Bridging your career and your creativity
Being creative in all departments
Acquiring learning habits
Opening up new routes
Games for success
Using the past in the present
Case study
Summary

10. Writing poems for yourself
Poems and being spontaneous
The poet's notebook
Generating images
Surprise and shock: inner stories
Practising the art of haiku
Case study
Summary

11. Telling stories for wholeness
Knowing stories as magic
Writing down dreams
Metanarratives: reading wider
Metanarratives: ourselves in stories
Parables for understanding
Case study
Summary

12. Bringing writing into the centre
Summary of progress: keeping subject files
Sharing it all: starting a read-write group
Applying the skills – beyond your journal
Brainstorming in the final workshop
Narratories into everyday life
Case Study
Summary

List of Illustrations

1	Your reader biography	13
2	A created profile	85
3	Map of imagination	160
4	Page of a poet's notebook	183
5	Example of a metanarrative	213

Introduction

Understanding Creativity in Your Life

I rhyme to set the darkness echoing... I rhyme to see myself
Seamus Heaney: *North*.

We make ourselves through words, and we change ourselves through more words. These words are individuated; we access them in our search for the richness of our life-experience and for the sustenance of our being in the world. As a writer and teacher, I have come to see that many people need help and guidance in the effort to understand that stock of words which lies dormant and which we call upon when we desire to explain who we are and what we want.

This book is not a magical spell for transforming blandness and discontent into something rich and strange. It is about how you can work creative thinking into your life in a way that will give a spiritual, instinctual quality to your life; it is concerned with the ways in which language is your most powerful tool for working out change and renewal. There are no formulae, but there are methods of cultivating what is there, dormant in you and in us all.

In my years as a teacher of creative writing and as a tutor for mature students, I have seen that a desire to get an education, to 'learn everything' as Willy Russell's Rita says, is often no more than something else in disguise: a lack of acceptance of what we are. This society instils in us a culture of success. We are told to look beautiful, to move gracefully, to perform so that we do well in interviews; we are told that certain body-shapes are acceptable, and that well-being is central to all quality of living.

There is nothing wrong with all this. It's just that something fundamental is overlooked. This is that element in being human which keeps us content and fulfilled even with the meanest, least materially successful life. This is the pool of silent, latent and perhaps infinite creative pleasure in our imaginations. How do we access this? Is it possible to live without recognising this, and if we try to do so, what are the penalties? People tend to think in terms of potential negativity, yet in fact, the search for those words which will enlighten ourselves with regard to our creative heart is actually fun. The word 'light-hearted' is a simple but accurate definition of the right attitude in this.

What can your words do to change your life?

The words you will use in the course of this book will be your own. They will be words packed with vibrancy and power, maybe latent, waiting to be used because you have not yet made space for them in your life.

- They can heal, often by making you stand back and see a problem for what it is
- They can fulfil your deepest needs for expression
- They can communicate the deepest feelings
- They can make sense of your own world and selfhood

I have seen a look of pleasure and joy on the face of a student of seventy who has just written her first poem in a class. I have watched a group of people work on a film script and discover that they have ideas to offer and that they can command language to influence others. I have seen people learn to trust their words, to feel their way towards seeing the sheer potency of eloquence in a situation. Words heal, words build and words persuade. They can lie and they can steal, but used rightly, words may give us the joy of self-expression and of releasing the knots of complexity which trouble us.

Research has shown that writing about the self and expressing our imagination can reduce stress. People who keep diaries or journals have often recorded how much the 'friend' (the diary page) is like a silent listener, another part of their self, quiet and receptive to certain truths which cannot be uttered in a normal day.

Write Your Self is a manual for encouraging that pool of creativity inside you. If you feel a sense of restlessness, even within a supposedly successful career or in a materialistic lifestyle, you may be certain that there is something else – something inside you like a place that you have known about and heard of but never visited. This manual is an itinerary of that place and a map directing you to a purposeful visit.

You will be asked to start a certain range of habits, all based on self-reflection and on logging aspects of yourself that perhaps you always took for granted. The renewals offered are like those feelings you have on holiday, when you discover a new, fascinating culture and you never want to leave and return to routine. Being truly creative can mean that you have no need of strategies against boredom, because you make a life that leaves no window for boredom. Thomas Gray, the poet, said that to be happy is to be perpetually employed. This means being active in all the best, fun-centred senses. Creativity is play. It means re-visiting not just a place but a playground.

To grasp the real potential of this book, do three things. These are the fundamentals of my course:

1. Write a journal.
2. Cultivate the poet in your spirit
3. Talk about, and write about, the *narratories* in your life. The concept of the narratory is central to the book. This concept is a term which describes all the story-making that has made you what you are, from bedtime stories when you were a child to your dream-fantasies as an adult. What I call a narratory is an assemblage of all these as a profile of yourself.

When you have finished the fun tasks in this manual, you will have met a stranger – a likeable stranger. That person will be you.

Finally, what will this book actually do to enrich your life?

- ♦ It will provide you with tools for shaping a better self-understanding
- ♦ It will show you how language makes sense of the world.
- ♦ It will shine a torch into the dark cave of your creative self

- It will empower you as a person in your social or business roles
- It will be fun to do, if you follow the exercises and feedback

CHAPTER 1

Taking Stock of the Raw Data

The public enemy number one of creativity is your dislike of yourself

Seeing your present creative potential

You are a human being and therefore your purposes here on earth are unknown, and there is no general rule about happiness. But your first duty is to be happy in your own way. You make your contentment by knowing yourself. As Socrates said, hundreds of years B.C., the beginning of wisdom is to admit that we know nothing. We might *know* nothing, but we *feel* thousands of things every day.

Creative thinking is about how we use and access these fragmentary senses of what we might have been, how we might have acted, what identities we might take up. You need to start at the point of liking yourself, and playing with your inner sense of the child. A useful first step is to ask yourself these questions:

- Do you make time for play – board-games, party-games, sport etc.

- Do you day-dream – and if so, do you see this as being silly?
- Do you often feel that you are not living the life you meant to live?
- Are you attracted to stories, soaps, novels, films etc. whenever you can make time?

If you feel that most of these apply to you, then consider the meanings of such habits. Notice how often people at work try to introduce playfulness – such as jokes, fooling around or talking about their children. Talk about holidays is often full of longing, as if work is merely an intermission between the holidays – which represent the real meaning of living. 'Purposes' in life, maybe expressed as 'aims and objectives' surprisingly tend to arrive most convincingly into our awareness when least expected. Hence the fascination of the moment of realization, the epiphany (in a non-religious sense) when your own truth opens up in the light, to be understood like never before.

Shaking off failure

Often, these habits reflect a deep need to play, to experiment and to revisit the mental landscapes of your childhood. It is the burden of failure which most inhibits this frustrated state of being, where you are stuck in a routine you have made in the false perception that it is what adults do, or it was considered " good job." The failure you might be feeling is mainly a failure to live in the fullest sense. Modern work-patterns allow us to use only a minute part of our vast human capabilities.

If you see your lifestyle as a failure because you have no time to express other aspects of yourself, how do you escape this feeling? You re-introduce playtime into your life. The coffee-break crossword is not enough. That poet in your spirit wants to sing, to celebrate life by smashing the ordered, the rational, the everyday patterns of imposed life.

> *Poetry is a way of showing us the beautiful truths in an ugly world. Creative living is using words to celebrate, to look at fragments as well as complete systems. We can all be poets because we all have a sense of what is beautiful for us.*

Starting your journal

Now you are to start the most important part of what should be an energising force for your life. This is your personal journal. The habit of journaling is based on no specific formula or layout. The important thing is to reflect on yourself each day, monitoring progress in understanding and creativity. A good journal has three main positive effects:

1. It forces you to reflect on habits and actions
2. It helps you to understand your ambitions, frustrations and abilities.
3. It provides a space for the 'other you' – the quiet self who remains the same beneath all the trials and demands of life your social self has to encounter.

Your commitment for the course

For this course, your journaling will be sufficient if you have two pages a day filled in, with these headings every time:

- Random responses to life
- Reflections on myself with others
- Notes on my new life

Your journaling will begin with this simple approach. After a few weeks, the material in your journal will also become to basis of the writing exercises in each chapter.

Random responses

Reader into Writer

But first you need to reflect on yourself as a creative being who has the potential to write well, with excitement and passion, with honesty and a genuine confrontation with the personal as well as the universal. Research has shown that all our reading, from being early readers as children, through to the random but often demanding reading of everyday adult lives, establishes our personal style. I would go further, and say that these habits make our responses to the world. Thinking and writing go together. Your reading shows you how to formulate those social discourses which make up the person that the world sees.

How do you access this reader in you, in order that you will better understand the growing writer, the manipulator of the words that will make your new life? The first step is to understand that so much in life flashes by in a blur, and that stopping to look properly, and to revise the past, is a huge asset in effecting the right kind of change.

A reader biography

A simple way to do this is to map out your biography as a reader. The summary on the following page shows you the processes of these questions. But first consider the ways in which you read and why you read. This is the basis of your contact with language used creatively. Your history as a reader provides the best clues to your potential talent as a writer. When you read, do you notice features of style and vocabulary? Do you find that really striking phrases and images will lodge in your mind and clamour for some attention?

Reading in our culture is often an oppositional process; it may even be stressful. There are always hurdles such as tests, set books and having to read very dull texts. You may associate reading with either very pleasant or very unpleasant experiences. For you, it may always have been an escape from reality rather than a way to understand it. This is all powerful potential material for the writer in you.

Active language-using

All these are good signs. It means that you are an active reader, and the chances are that there is an urge in you to write. The writing you should have in mind is first of all for yourself. The subject here is not publication. The course you are now following is one that is entirely private and personal to you. When you re-read what you have produced, the purpose will be an enlightenment of yourself.

Remember that creative writing, or even letter-writing, lightens burdens, releases muddled feelings and encourages an honest confrontation with problems. Sometimes it can even point out problems you never knew you had.

The point is that language has to be active, renewing, always taking you into fresh imaginative dimensions. If your words go stale, then so do you. Think how many times, in everyday talk, you find yourself thinking 'Did I actually say that?'

Every handbook on successful interview techniques stresses the need for personality the come through. What else is personality but something made of your language mixing with your essential self?

Move on to the reader biography now, and write short answers or lists for each question. The idea with this is that you understand the changes in your patterns of life in which you have hungered for the creative food which the best writing supplies. Try to list details of how, why and where you read or used to read when a child.

Successes/happy associations	obstacles/fears	examples of texts read
Stage one: early years, learning to read (say 4-8 years old)		

e.g. stories you read/heard that gave you pleasure.	teachers/tests?	Stories/comic strips etc.

Stage two: reading at exam time/ early teens

Things you read despite tests Or 'set books'	GCSE exams?	List your loves/hates
	Having to read novels for tests	
Cult novels		
Alternative humour etc.		

Stage three: current reading

Time to indulge in reading?	No time.	List your loves/hates
Reading books recommended by friends?	Time only for career	
Texts mentioned in reviews etc.	professional texts.	

Fig. 1   Your reader biography

Summarising notes

When you have written notes in all these columns, write a few words in the final box, summing up your current feelings about you and your relationship to your reading time and habits. You might discover that, as a child, you were always told you were 'good at English' and that you stopped the reading habits when career thoughts stepped into your life. Maybe you could make time to read those influential novels you keeping hearing about.

Developing the ideas further

Think about this person in you who has assumed the role of reader since being very young. Has this person been passive? Has the reading usually been for a purpose you now recognise or has your reading only ever been directed by someone else? Follow up the exercise even more by writing a page of your journal reflecting on these aspects of the reader in you:

- The extent to which you have been empowered as a reader
- Are you now an independent reader who thinks about language?
- Consider how far you discuss what you have read with others
- Think about the choices in your reading – the restrictions. What has formed your taste in this? Have you been adventurous, or are you stuck in the same categories? Write that page in your journal, challenging yourself on these issues.

Educating yourself emotionally

There has been a recent vogue for what some writers have called 'emotional intelligence'. I am not asking you to take part in some kind of inverted IQ test. I am referring to some notable aspects of what people need to do in order to prepare to write. Preparation is of three kinds:

1. The basic command of language and the confidence that comes with this.
2. The awareness of what your subject is to be.
3. The honest and profound looking into yourself.

The first one is all about the warm feeling of self-belief – that you write fluently and well even though the result may simply be a letter to the bank manager. This is all good, and will be a huge resource for you later on.

The second one is hard. It demands that you think long and hard about the kind of subjects and styles that suit you best. For this, you need to log your interests in popular culture and media. For instance, if you follow plots and character in 'soaps' then the chances are you will write fiction. If you like factual documentaries and biographies, then perhaps factual writing, with research, is right for you. The sure way to find out is to write instinctively first of all, then see what you have.

The third one is really testing and asks you to search into the kind of person you are, fundamentally. A human is a bundle of complexities. As a species, we tend to disguise feeling and spontaneous response in order to follow convention, not to 'lose face' and to fulfil social roles or even gender-functions within relationships and families.

But have you even asked yourself the kind of basic questions that an interviewer would ask you if they wanted a profile of the elements in you that brought satisfaction, made you laugh, made you indignant, caused you deep pain? For the kind of writing in the following chapters, you will need to do this now. Begin by opening your journal at the first blank page, and write two lists. For instance:

What creates feelings of love in me	*What disturbs my equilibrium*

You might list:

Watching children play	Having to walk past city beggars
Looking at family photographs	Seeing images of suffering on television
Simple pleasures like shopping	feeling helpless or ashamed.

The list could continue and be a very long one. My point is that by spending half an hour on this, and filling one page of your notebook, you will have the beginnings of a profile of yourself as a thinking, feeling, responding person, with all the paradoxes and fantasies that modern existence brings with it. Yet this is also the foundation of your writing. Consider what possible whirlwinds of feelings you might have passing that beggar:

He's pretending. He has a car around the corner.

I have ten pounds in my pocket. It's staying there – for bread and stamps.

I'm not going to even look at him.

My God.... He has no shoes. Sixteen years old, same as my John..

These oppositional forces make the inner creative clashes which make thoughts, shapes and words of our feelings. Do not let them float away. Monitor them in your notebook. Note them mentally and write them down later in the day.

All this is your first material for the **Random responses to life** heading in the journal.

Being a child, seeing as a child

This first chapter has been concerned with some approaches to accessing the playfulness, the whimsicality of the child we all still have inside. You can develop this by thinking, as you write notes, about a child's perspectives. Notice how similar these are to much innovative writing and art :

An innocent eye

Spontaneity

Lack of inhibition

Response to play

Sensitivity to the whole environment

A need for solitude and a need for company

These are all elements in the creative process. How do you access them in order to write? A simple first step is to observe children at play and write random notes. Log the things they say and their observations. The child in the pushchair will notice a cloud-shape and say, 'Look, camel!' The adult may never even look at the sky, as he or she is thinking of the gas bill.

You could even try to express, simply in lists, the perspectives on the world from four feet of height. Think of the joy of any unusual perspective, as in the scene in the film *Dead Poets' Society* where the English teacher (played by Robin Williams) asks his class to stand on their desks and consider their little world from that point of view. The young men in the class giggle like children in a playground.

In fact, the metaphor of the playground is exactly right. Make your routine like a journey interrupted by playground enjoyment. Never resist a natural expression of play, fun, chat or sharing with others, if that is what your instinct tells you to do. Most of all, take time. In the streets, never walk like to busy, purposeful businessperson. The French nineteenth century city poets of Baudelaire's time had a word, 'flaneur' – this was the artist who strolled, who took in all observations and had time to really apply the senses to the material world. Children very rarely glance at watches and time seems endless to them in most cases. Time is a concept made for prisons.

> *Oscar Wilde said we should make our lives like a work of art. Why not make them like buildings with limitless rooms, all waiting to be furnished by imagination? Cultivate your mental visioning and fill the spaces.*

Escaping the sheer burden of time-awareness is something we all know and value, but usually we only taste that delicious light of freedom for a few moments. Cultivating the art of the *flaneur* is one of the basics of creative life: a good start in this is to walk around a circumscribed space (a few streets, a piece of rural landscape) giving an adjective to he feature or item before you that most attracts interest. A few single words of that kind will lead to others, as in the old, traditional formula of 'words make sentences, sentences make paragraphs and wow, you have an essay.'

Reflections

Exercise one

Now it is time for the first actual writing exercise, rather than the random notes you have been asked to write so far. Each exercise (one in each chapter) is intended to encourage your quiet, passive and changeless self to emerge. The exercises should each be about 600 words in length, and written in a companion notebook to your journal. Also date the writing exercises, as you should do the journal entries also.

Defamiliarising: In a famous statement about literature, a Russian writer said that writing should make the stone stony. It should show the essential stone-quality of the stone. Yet, strangely, writing that 'stony' nature also makes the object less familiar – because we have to look afresh. What was said above about a child's perception applies here. You have to *consider how you could write about yourself from the outside*, from a fresh viewpoint, bringing out the essential of your observed life. When you simply describe a car, for instance, you take for granted all the details and functions. But think about how a tribesman from a culture which has no car would put the perception of the car into words. Perhaps 'moving box making roaring sound'.

The exercise is this: write about yourself as if you are composing a letter written by a neighbour who has watched you at work. Your 600 words should be in the form of this letter, but you are the main subject of the piece, seen in this fresh way.

Remember, one of the foundations of creative writing is to observe what is there, not what society or habit or belief says is there. This applies to your life as much as to a government or a tower-block.

You should find this quite enlightening with regard to how others see you, and also you should ask *how you think that others see you*. The point of this first exercise is to show you that in standing back from yourself and the routine life you are always immersed in is a path to understanding. Your answer to this question should make you stand back and think 'Say, this is me taking a few paces away from myself and watching.' So what did you see?

You might want to make it humorous. A common answer is to use gentle, undermining satire and irony about oneself, as in a letter to a relative. This is fine. It's a positive sign that you can laugh at yourself and see this as a strength.

It may be that you simply describe yourself through these alien eyes. This has advantages also. Reading through your objective account should make you see how defamiliarising relates to the point about seeing like a child. The point is that you look at yourself as if you are a stranger, with all the wonderment and curiosity we all feel when watching another person for the very first time. The familiar is also the alluring, the glamorous. Bear in mind that even in Samarkand, someone has to empty the bins. The dreaming poet and the bin-person see the place very differently.

Feedback and Discussion

What you have done, as your first writing exercise, is look at yourself through imagined perceptions. In other

words, you have made fiction so that truth can get a little closer.

Exercise 1 has achieved these writing objectives:

- Started the habit of self-reflection
- Made you stand back and understand yourself afresh
- Given you an insight into the fictional habit of 'let's pretend'

The value of this standing outside also introduces the notion of seeing how writing closes up on the raw data of life. That *data* in this case is you. Creativity with language is fundamentally about using the idea of 'making the stone stony'. That is, getting as close as possible to the actual nature of your being, or the object's observed condition. Notice how in fiction we love to judge characters, based on information given, and that we 'create' things about fictional people, using our experience of life.

Just as fiction is a test of life, your writing is a test of your self-knowledge. So writing a new life for yourself, based on the journal and the exercises here, involves gradually coming closer to that understanding of **your** essential qualities. These are very unlikely to be the qualities given to you by parents, schoolteachers, siblings or employers. These words of yours will approach a being who has been neglected, ignored, categorised or even labelled by some kind of system or patterning.

Notes

Following up

For all these reasons, the next stage in the journaling is to write something about how others have seen you, defined you. For instance, what person does your employer/partner/brother/sister etc. *want* to see? From your letter exercise, now write more freely about the various persons you are in the world, using categories based on:

You at home

You at work

You inside a family role

Case Study

Jenny was nearing forty and all her life was meetings, ansaphone messages and e-mail. Some days it felt as if her dreams of being a 'full person' had dissolved into chores, routine and a sense of information overload. Her evenings were often spent reading reports so that she was ready for the next day's meetings. It was taking half an hour each morning simply to answer e-mails, keep up with Facebook, write a blog, and so on.

Where was the other life? Where was that other Jenny who used to love jazz, go to theatre, have time for a long lunch with friends? That had been Jenny the student. And that was too long ago to contemplate with a sense of equanimity.

One day in September, she noticed a poster listing the evening-class subjects on offer at the local college. Her attention was caught by the words 'Self expression'. It was a creative writing course, and if it promised such a thing, then why not give it a try? The notion of her 'self' seemed beyond her grasp at that moment.

The first class was sheer fun. They played word-games, no more. The exercises forced her to search for that enquiring mind of the undergraduate, when she had talked about new words and new concepts. At home, she took down the dictionary from the shelf and looked up some words that people has said in class. Just skimming the dictionary made Jenny realise how much she was not using.

The first step, and it was one she could take at work the next day, was to start a conversation about politics, and that was to be the basis of next week's writing. It was a challenge, but she purposely took a coffee-break and talk with Ron and Sue about the European parliament. It was clear that they all loved it, and had all been bursting to express some of the massive amount of information aimed at them from screens, paper and images in every working day.

Summary of development so far:
This chapter has opened the way for you to see how changing perspectives on yourself is in itself a primary creative move. The exercises covered are about ways of shifting perception and seeing afresh, often with the bias or innocence of others. Simply escaping the too familiar is a guaranteed recipe for a creative springboard. Remember that class with Robin Williams, standing on their desks to look afresh.

- You are to keep a journal for random notes, using the three headings given.
- You are going to write at random, and cultivate thinking like a child when looking at the world
- Your reading should be directed and prioritised to help you as a writer.

- Your targets should be to bring your imagination out from the shadows, and play with its innocent, whimsical tastes.
- Every observation should be like the first. Note and reflect on all details that attract your attention. This is defamiliarising what is too familiar.

CHAPTER 2

Making Other Selves from Your Present Self

You have now started a specific set of writing habits and these are your foundation for progress. The next stage is to think more purposefully about the whole idea of journaling. This is simply a modern development of the traditional act of keeping a diary, but several writers and psychologists have noted the ways in which logging your development and self-knowledge can be done in this basic daily expression of ideas, images and feelings. It is important not to discount anything: what comes through, wanting to be expressed in words, will of course be filtered, edited, but don't discount the material itself.

Journaling for Self-Insights

Why is keeping a journal so important in beginning writing your new life? The plain answer is that recent developments in the art have shown that it has all the aspects of self-knowledge we need. It is so comprehensive that it may contain notes on your past formative experiences, your present state of being and indeed your desired future for yourself. The journal pages are yours only- a secret covenant if you like; a place for the kind of expression that everyday reality tends to eclipse.

A journal is flexible. There are no rules about how the writing should be structured. Remember that you can't be *wrong* in these exercises. You are in control, and the only person who need ever read your words is yourself. You don't need to worry about correct English either. Just write what you feel in the way you want to. There is no-one with a red pen about to assess your powers of language.

As you acquire the best habits of journaling, notice what things you tend to do which are departures from the familiar everyday self you thought you knew. Keeping a journal will encourage you to break away from the too-familiar. The pages have a kind of depth – they can expand or deepen into sheer imagination, if that's where you want to go in your writing about yourself.

Purposes of Journaling:

- ♦ To take time for reflection
- ♦ To record what is important in your personal growth
- ♦ To make a basis for revising your self-knowledge

- To meditate on the nature of all experience: good and bad
- To refine your relationship to your own words

Choose the right notebook for you

This journal is going to be the basis of all your imagining and creativity, so make it right for you. It doesn't have to be expensive or bound in leather. But it needs to be quite large. An A4 page will be adequate. Also, you should find it easier to use if it is not lined. This is because a blank page gives you a sense of freedom – an invitation to doodle or sketch if need be, to enhance the words. You might want some words in large letters or capitals, or even include a poem. A blank page makes all this easier.

Most people recommend a bound book rather than a spiral-notebook. It has a feel of permanence and solidity. One possibility might be that you could write on the right-hand side (recto) and add additional things later on the left (verso). The choice is yours. A cheap notebook or diary from the local newsagent can be fine if you are comfortable in using it.

Also, a pencil is preferred to a pen for journaling by some writers, as they claim that it feels less formal and academic. But again, try fountain pen, ball pen and pencil until you are happy. The obvious things like comfort in the hand and a good grip are also important, so experiment and find what is workable.

> *Like all proper tools, a writing implement should be right, feel right, be a part of you so that you sense a closeness to what goes on paper.*

Now is a good time to try the first journal piece. You should reflect on what influences have most formed the person you are today. Consider the people who have been important to you, such as parents, teachers, close friends or even favourite writers or artists. What aspects of you do you do you think are established because of these influences?

Random responses- influences on you

Start by bringing to mind these formative influences, in categories of:

People

Ideas

Experiences

Works of art/imagination

Simply brainstorm a list at first, and then do a ranking exercise, picking out the most important one from each list. In this way, you might have (a) Your best friend (b) a belief in God (c) a traumatic experience from which you recovered (d) Shakespeare

Your random reflections are simply to write a short account of what you owe to, or how you gained from, the item on the list. An example might be:

Best friend:

From Julie I have learned that real friendship allows you a chance to be totally honest, with a firm sense of trust. Julie and I tell each other all our little problems. We laugh off most worries, but when the deeper ones remain, we can usually help by listening, and by giving the kind of help that only someone who knows the other well can give. I know I have someone there I can rely on. She has given me a sense of belonging and love.

Writing about the Journey so far

The way to develop from this tentative beginning is to consider your life so far as a long climb up a mountain. What point do you instinctively feel that you have reached?

The mountain has foothills, gentle slopes and meadows; then it rises more steeply, offering more challenges and more effort. After that the going might be really tough, scrambling up gullies. Or of course, your mountain might have been easier. Have you had a sense of climbing it alone, or have you always been part of a team?

Your climb may have been filled with the apprehension of a fall, with no party around, providing ropes, safety-nets and even encouragement. But perhaps your climb has been all an easy matter, with the summit clearly in view. It might be useful to recall here also, that in fear and apprehension lies the thrill of the adventure as well.

Free writing

As you write in your new journal, just let your thought have a free flow. When you write about that mountain-climb, let the thoughts and feelings come out honestly and openly. There are no constraints. Your journal page is going to become a friend, a listener, a multi-dimensional place where imagination goes unchecked. There is no-one to argue back and undermine your interpretations of the journey. No-one ever said that the journey is bad if it has been too easy.

Free or automatic writing is a valuable tool for writing new dimensions about yourself. This is because the idea is to write without rational thought. Simply let all random words, phrases and images flow from you. At this stage, this is just to see what happens, for fun. Later on, it will be developed further.

You might want to approach the 'mountain journey' exercise in this way. The choice is yours. Just remember that there are no certainties in how people interpret these free-flow writings. They may have no profound significance at all. The words may only reflect a sense of play in you – a need to be whimsical and let your imagination loose on the data of everyday life.

Writing about Now

The next stage in making new 'selves' , fresh dimensions on the complexity which is in all humans, is to work up to writing with a more definite purpose, with clearer guidelines. The best place to start is by considering yourself at this specific moment in time. Too often in modern life we have the sense that accelerating change is leaving us behind. The processes of communication, on both a domestic and on a global scale, are so formidable that it is easy to feel a sense of awe.

This makes a feeling of being significant, or of achieving something tangible, increasingly difficult. If your ambitions are limited to the areas of career and money, then it may be that too much of your attention is given up to dwelling on time yet to come rather than on *this time* now.

Capturing this moment

As with meditation in Eastern philosophies, so with journaling, one of the central objectives is to look into each moment of time and maximise it. You may find that you are so preoccupied with planning ahead that now escapes you. There are some signs that tell you something about your attitude to valuing time for yourself:

- Writing lists almost everyday, listing your aims
- Setting impossible tasks
- Leaving out social time when work deadlines beckon
- Not noticing people around you
- Always seeing things from your own viewpoint
- Avoiding conversations because of scheduled time

Of course, many of these have a positive side. But recall what was said earlier about walking the streets with an eye to detail, and to observing the magic of the ordinary. Many writers keep a pocket book in which they write character notes and fragments of overheard conversation. Your journal could include these in your 'notes' section, but for now, just consider the possibilities of this moment.

Give yourself twenty minutes for this, and simply think about the people in your life at this very moment, bringing to mind what they will be doing now, and what they might be saying, and to whom; what they might be wearing and what thoughts might be in their minds. You could include best friends, relatives, even people you once knew and have lost touch with. Then think of places that are important to you. Bring those places to mind. Simply list these things at random.

Certain aspects of your attitudes to time will emerge from this. Did you find it easy to bring detail into focus? Or did you struggle to picture the place? For example, the place where your partner works: how well do you know or imagine that to be? The point is that we are all caught in the tangled undergrowth of our own concerns, our everyday duties and chores. This is made more dense and potentially choking if the demands of our planned future are added. Now becomes lost and time shoots by.

Your mind may be always striving to find its fulfilment. You may be conditioned to educate, to gain more and more skills in order to survive in this information society. But what about the little voice of the self, calling out to be heard in the cacophony of wants and desires? This self is strongly related to that part of us which writes, manipulates words into meanings. This is why 'making other selves' means, for the present purposes, recognising your impulses to have these freedoms:

1. To imagine other worlds
2. To understand negativity
3. To accept that you are several 'selves' in the sense of human hunger for meaning.
4. To see language as a way to contentment as well as protest.

Being a Poet of your 'Little universe'

Now it's time to move towards a solid piece of writing in your journal, based on your thinking about self and time. The medieval and renaissance world saw humans as microcosms ('little worlds') reflecting the giant cosmos of the universe. You are, as a writer working for a new life for your fundamental self, such a 'little universe' of meanings and for this exercise you are to write imaginatively about the complexities of yourself.

Think about something you are learning to do right now. Write down a description of what this is, and how you are having to adapt to it. Then reflect on your attitude to that learning, and what others do in response. For instance, if you were learning to play classical guitar you might find:

(a) Learning to use your hands differently was the key skill – using muscles in wrist and fingers which are not used to being stretched.

(b) Your mental attitudes to this might include protest (why do I bother when there is pain?) or even little triumphs when you play the right note.

(c) Your son or brother or friend might laugh – thinking you want to be Segovia in three easy lessons.

Put all these levels of thinking and feeling together in one piece. Assessing the complexities of you as you grow, develop and change.

A neat way to do this, is as a simple poem with these phrases:

I laugh with triumph when…. / I rage inside when………
My little world is on its axis when….. / My world is hit by meteors when…….

Simply put lists of things to complete the statements.

> Trying to understand your self can be tougher than tackling advanced maths. After all, there is no textbook and certainly no formula.

Writing Dialogues

Another aspect of this effort to acknowledge and understand the many 'selves' inside, pulling against your main objectives, or perhaps asking too much of your limited strength and resources, is the need to find balance and a healthy routine. Writing enables you to see more clearly the drives of the thwarted imagination inside you.

We all have this hunger for our imaginative life to flower, to be given space in the everyday timetable of work. Your first journaling exercises have started this process, but there is another aspect of these conflicting voices all wanting fulfilment. This is our expression of what we *do not* say or write. Of course, merely writing dialogue also tests our knowledge of others, too, as we work for a sense of authenticity. This is why, in fiction, dialogue seeming 'real' is so important.

Dialogues against fear and taboo

The literary idea of the 'stream of consciousness' as in the novels of Virginia Woolf for instance, concerns the expression of the inner voices which roam around our minds all the time, in both important and trivial settings. The familiar experience of being in a meeting and the 'mind wandering' as attention fades is an instance of this. Think of the different voices within you and what they say.

This is where actually writing your dialogues becomes a fruitful exercise. These may take a variety of forms, depending on your state of mind or whether you are experiencing stress, anxiety or any particularly strong emotion:

- Answers to things which frighten you
- Nagging doubts
- 'Devil's Advocate' voices undermining you
- Urges to escape or hide
- The voices of sheer emotion

These are all related to feelings of discontent or to entertainment. They are, of course, often related to your boredom threshold, and it's that child in you again, wanting to play, to experience change and challenge.

Notes

Complete this phase of your writing with some snatches of dialogue which capture the most persistent 'inner conversations' you might have – your preoccupations. They might be such ordinary things as:

'You really must get that plumbing job done…'

'Why? Can't afford it anyway.'

Or more important things such as:

'Really, get organised. You have to sit down tonight and sort out the wardrobe. Then get jogging. You know you want that new dress to fit you…'

'Oh, I'm too tired. I'll start the new regime tomorrow.'

I know someone who calls the inner voice that always wants to rest, to unwind, to leave until tomorrow 'Fat John'. Fat John is the John who wants to come in from work and sit in front of the television, without a wash or a change of clothes.

These notes will be about your unacknowledged restlessness, and they form a basis of a great deal of vibrant, insightful writing.

Case Study

Tony was going through a phase of being unsettled at work. His job as a Tax Officer was fine in many ways, but he was beginning to feel one-sided and in need of something different. By writing a brainstorming list of his nagging complaints as well as his emotional fancies and dreams, he gradually put together a summary of his discontents.

As the centre of all this seemed to be the fact that he had never stopped to ask whether he was happy or fulfilled. He had gone from school to college then into a career without 'finding himself'. He had ignored his physical side: that fact that he was a powerful swimmer, and then when he was younger he had done some quite demanding camping and climbing expeditions in Scotland.

He wrote about these frustrations, and he actually put on paper the delights and satisfaction he had felt when out in the wilds. By describing these things, he became more fully aware of that aspect of himself, and felt a clearer sense of what he had to re-discover – and also how he might do it.

Summary

This chapter has been an introduction to how writing can be an art with the potential to make reflecting on your life a positive and creative action, with often revolutionary results. The topics covered have been intended to help you make positive reflections on yourself as a reader and writer, and to give you that initial confidence you need to carry on. You have been asked to make a start with a long process of self-examination, but not in any solemn way. The underpinning skills you have acquired are these:

- Using a journal for self-knowledge strategies
- Writing about your sense of self
- How writing can clarify discontents
- Understanding the importance of relishing the moment
- Using strategies like dialogues and lists to understand inner 'selves'

CHAPTER 3

Escaping the Catharsis Trap

This chapter moves on to consider some ways of avoiding the negativity implicit in journaling and logging thoughts and feelings. For instance, how often do you meet people who say they tried to keep a diary but stopped when it became just an outlet for complaints and dissatisfactions? It is too easy for developmental writing to become concerned with these gripes, as outlets for frustrations and feelings of failure.

Again, we return to the question: why is writing misery so much easier than writing joy? It sounds like a proposition for debate, and so it may well be, but at present, the assumption may be taken and exploited for your advantage- in other words, write the joy. The fact that this is hard is all the more rewarding when complete.

Knowing your feelings honestly

The first step towards making this course of writing totally creative, revitalising and forward-looking is to cancel out the idea that such writing is only about cleaning our bad feelings. In classical Greece, when the philosopher Aristotle reflected on tragic drama, he used the word *catharsis* to describe that peculiar feeling we have of being emotionally wrung out after seeing or reading a story of intense suffering.

Catharsis literally means a 'cleansing' of excess emotion. It has a place in this book, but for now, avoid focusing on this in your writing. Everyone knows the obvious instances of this: a funeral is a good example. Notice how difficult it is for people to think of anything to say about the deceased at first; there is often a tense and silent period of time. Everyone feels strained and uneasy. Then someone breaks the ice and there is a general feeling of release: people are free to talk and even humour is allowed. Expressions of love and affection, and the attractions of happy memories all figure in this. A certain catharsis has taken place in that release.

Why is this so important?

The emotional life is the very core of everything in creative writing and in its developmental role in particular. Think of all the potential oppositions to our honest expression of our feelings. Why else do we read fiction and watch films so much if not to examine the emotional life of individuals, and compare it with our own? There are so many hurdles on the course towards winning the war against direct and frank expression of that inner life.

This list stresses the range of opposition here, all the factors working against our expression of emotion:
- Fear of embarrassment or failure
- Uncertainty about how you will be understood
- 'Stiff Upper Lip' attitudes
- Difficulties in finding the 'right' words

But there are writing strategies which help here. The root causes of these difficulties are largely linked to our understanding of ourselves. A person who is totally confident in expressing feelings and responses has no fear of offending others, nor of appearing stupid, nor even of being labelled in some way. Children do it all the time. They have no complex notions about how they are perceived.

But adults have gone through the many processes of being defined by others, by the 'System' or by families and relationships. When an occasion comes along which demands this emotional expression, we often fail because there are too many inner lines of thought about concepts of ourself. How do we overcome this?

Reflections

One method, with writing as your tool, is to work towards a composite picture of yourself as a self that relates to the feelings *expected of you,* as compared to the spontaneous responses you feel in your inner urges.

This is the exercise to highlight this in your journaling, following three stages.

Stage one

Bring to mind a situation from your past in which you had to talk about your feelings of suffering or stress. Write a short description of that situation, including where you were, whether it was formal, or at home or work etc. Explain to yourself what the subject was.

Stage two

Now list the constraints: what were the factors which made the talk difficult? For instance, it might have been your lack of knowledge about the listener; it might have been your inability to utter the actual words inside, or maybe it was simply that you were in the wrong place, or it was the wrong time of day. Maybe you had no privacy, or you felt ill at the time, and so on.

Stage three

Finally, list the actions you could take to make sure that the right words would be said, should a similar occasion arise in the future. *Actually write the words you wanted to say at the time.*

Learning Narratories

We now come to one of the core concepts of this book. You have just been thinking about the constraints on your expression of emotion. Have you ever thought about the definitions made about that person who is you? The point here is that we are all told who we are by a whole range of people who tell us who we are, what we are good at, how we should talk, react and so on.

Think about the long list of accounts written and spoken about you and who you are. This could be anything from a school report to your best friend who tells you that you are a poor dancer. A *narratory* is the sum of all these self-stories. Imagine a typical person in society now. How does he or she see and judge their self? What formative stories have been told about them, and how?

An example of a narratory
Here is the narratory of the Anonymous Citizen we shall call Person B:

Person B

Story one:

B is very good at English and so should be good at everything, but he has difficulties with practical skills, and has failed to impress in metalwork. He also shows no flair for games and has not participated in any team sports this year.

Story two:

B is always doing something else when you plan a night out. She never seems to want any social life. I mean, can you remember a staff night out when she's been there? B needs to get a life – I mean, all she talks about is that dog of hers and how they go for long walks.

Story three:

You don't like holidays abroad do you B? Let's forget Spain. You wouldn't like it. I know you always go for a quiet time by the sea at some quiet English resort. A good break for you is time to read and do a few crosswords – right?

Story four:

I have attended several courses on Information Technology, and I have two 'A' levels. Currently I am learning to drive and I have a reasonable fluency in French. I feel that your vacant post would enable me to develop my interests in retail management. I communicate well, and I think of myself as a useful and co-operative member of a team.

Person B's narratory has much more than these constituents, but these examples represent some of the dominant narratories told about us (and by ourselves) in society now.

> *Tell me what you read, what stories excite you, and I will know who you are and where you want to go in life.*

Your narratory is extremely diverse and puzzling. You will never know its fullness. All that is possible is to learn from the most powerful ones. For instance, were you ever labelled, in your childhood, as being 'difficult' or were words like 'loner' or 'rebel' stuck on you like badges?

Phases of Life

Your narratory changes as you develop in life and go through phases of growth. To see this, all you need to do is recollect your own contributions to the narratory. In other words, think about how you explain yourself. This is an ideal subject for your writing journal.

Responses

Start by writing an account of how you would write about your life in terms of significant achievement, as if you were doing a graph of your life so far. What would the watersheds be? The determining elements? This is a perfect point at which to chart the ways in which you value what you have achieved. Set out the writing with this structure:

1.

Achievements reflecting significant turning-points or changes (list them with dates)

2.

Write about your feelings now with regard to these.

3.

Now write about them as a narratory: that is, as you would define their importance in relation to your sense of value.

Example

You might think of doing a good interview that led to a job you value highly.

1. The job is one with responsibility, and it challenges and extends me. It has shown me that I am able to cope with pressure.
2. I often feel that the stress is too much to bear, but the sense of achievement outweighs these negative sensations.
3. The narratory would be:

' If I am honest, only a small part of me and my abilities is ever used in this work. In order to do the work well, I have to cancel out important aspects of my wishes, dreams and desires. But the part of my story it tells is Paul the manager, Paul who copes, Paul who wears a smart suit and feels good in it.'

Writing narratories about fears

So many of these stories which create us as social beings are basically part of a whole fabric of fears. Anyone could list the things in life they fear, but for many people now, high on the list would surely be fear of failure. We live in a society in which success is paramount. Notice how the phrase 'get a life' and the idea of someone being 'sad' if they differ from certain norms are becoming universal as means of reinforcing conformity.

The fear of failure is of course linked to the fear of not conforming – for most of us, who are most likely very well-conditioned 'good citizens'. But think more deeply about these fears. Narratories are created about them – often by ourselves. A perfect example of how deeply this runs can be gleaned from almost any television advert. Most adverts work on the principle of fear: this is a fear which creates a need. Makers of a kitchen detergent will persuade us that we should fear bacteria. The story of ourselves as people who will not tolerate bacteria is adding to your personal narratory.

In other words, there must be ways of sorting out exactly which aspects of your self are compose of actual fears, and which are illusions or delusions. An example might be a person who dreads non conforming, for instance in a student community. The reasons for that conformity are easy to list:

A desire to be accepted

A need to be 'modern'

A need to share a certain cultural identity

A search for real friendships

An escape from loneliness

But what about your deep-seated fears? How can writing a narratory help to remove them or place them in a healthy perspective? A direct method here is one that was established in medieval Japan by the court ladies who wrote 'pillow books'. These were an early version of a personal journal. The most famous is the pillow book of Sei Shonagon, written in tenth century Japan. She developed the habit of writing about things which disturbed her, and then explained why. For instance, she heads one page 'Nothing can be worse' and then lists things such as the appearance and behaviour of servants. She writes about decorum and proper social behaviour.

Your fears may not be so grand, but the point is to describe them, and then write about yourself and the fear *from a second perspective.*

<u>Fear</u>: Being seen as odd because I spend hours making model planes and ships

<u>Narratory</u>: This might be talk in the family: general teasing about it. Maybe being called a 'kid with his toys'. The hobby may not be seen as a 'macho' one etc.

The narratory is gradually built up in family small-talk and teasing. But it imprints itself on your subconscious.

<u>Second perspective</u>

I make models because I have loved the craft involved, ever since I was a child. I find that it is relaxing, and prevents me running through the events of the day and perhaps developing stressful thoughts and preoccupations. I also feel a profound pleasure in finishing the models. I think them to be beautiful artefacts and the displays can be most attractive and impressive,

This same approach could be used of far more important fears, such as a fear of speaking your mind, or being thought selfish and so on.

What the Greeks thought- cleansing things
This is now the right place to return to the idea of catharsis we discussed at the opening of this chapter. You have a mind full of these contributory stories now, and the power of that narratory which defines you has to be understood. So you have to decide which stories making up your narratory have to go. There are several reasons why they should be cleansed away:
- They may be distorted
- They perhaps define only the surface of you
- They may be dominated by your past self/selves
- They may say nothing of your emotional life

- They may say nothing of your intellectual life

List about six of the main stories you see in your narratory. Then delete the ones you want to erase. Underline the ones you think are accurate and valuable to you. Then start to think seriously and deeply about why the wrong ones have to go.

This is a catharsis. You must wash these distortions out of you. They may go way back to your childhood in a family or school context. You actually need to write the features of the bad stories, as in this example:

<u>Story</u>: When a child, I was thought to be clumsy and useless with manual work – by my family. I was known as Klutz and dad said that I would never even learn how to wire a plug or knock a nail in wood without hitting my thumb.

Correcting for your <u>narratory:</u>

Since being married last year, I have done several DIY jobs around the house. I have done some painting and wallpapering; I have proved that I can assemble a self-assembly desk, and I have used a power-drill. The Klutz has done. The Klutz was a lie – a story that has to be deleted.

You place it in the waste-bin, as if you are using your computer. The important part of this thinking is to write the words that you genuinely feel about the story you are deleting. Let the anger out, as if you were answering back to those who told that story. They unwittingly played a part in writing a narratory about you that has no relation to the truth. You see the truth, now, with experience and hindsight. Use your journal to write back, as if the storytellers you speak to are really there.

This kind of catharsis is a setting right; your words will be putting the record straight about yourself: correcting an injustice, a distortion that has perhaps persisted for far too long. The worst thing about these distortions is that they squat in your spirit like nasty nagging voices; like a howling dog who needs to be released into the open air. Journaling will clean and release, letting your genuine narratory establish itself. You want a narratory written with truth.

Your writing habit is now shaping up towards a fluent account of your creative and spiritual nature. The very act of writing in a journal is a creation of a defined space for language, a kind of sacredness, private to you and only you.

Creating different points of view

A story that forms part of someone's narratory is, of course, a point of view. It is only opinion or supposition. This is why so many of these contributory stories are dangerously distorted and oversimplified. A case in point would be biography. Choose three biographies written about a famous person and notice the immense differences; the example of the poet Keats is an illustration. He has been defined as a sensitive, delicate man, a well-trained medical man who saw great suffering; a poor rejected lover and a Romantic poet writing in a garret. These are all excessive perspectives, each with a grain of truth.

Your life is the same. Various people on your journey into life so far have assessed you and made value judgements about you in certain roles. But who can make a fundamental judgement? Only you yourself, and only then after some considerable effort and acceptance of some hard facts.

A useful strategy in writing on this is to purposely create other points of view about you by brainstorming across a whole range, and then ranking these in order of their closeness to what you see as the true you.

Notes

For this piece of writing, write the list first – a list of all your main roles in life – like this:

Wife, sister, nurse, musician, best friend, driver, listener...

Now rank these in order of their importance *for you*

Supposing you put 'best friend' first. Your writing task is now to write about yourself as a friend *as if you were your best friend.* So you write about yourself in the second person, using he/she.

She is a close friend because we talk about very private things,. And I can speak to her as I can with no other person, even my husband in some ways. She always gives me attention and listens to me, even if she is under considerable strain at the time we talk..... (and so on).

Notice how these notes shift the point of view and force you to think about yourself more deeply. These are some of the benefits of this exercise:

- Probing more deeply into your motivations
- Understanding your strengths and limitations
- Seeing through others' eyes
- Facing up to problems
- Expressing nagging discontents
- Reflecting on attitudes you may have assumed but not understood

Case Study

Jane was well established in her new job as a lecturer in further education. She was teaching mature students and feeling very fulfilled in the work. But a point came when she realised that talk and thought about her work were filling all her life. When she went out to dinner with friends or her partner, she seemed to talk of nothing but her students, her lesson ideas, and how much paperwork there was.

She was actually aware of this, but couldn't stop the intensity of her talk on the subject. It was such an easy way to communicate and made her feel important, and explained her work as something worthwhile. But one evening at a party, she overheard two friends talking about her. They expressed the opinion that she had become boring, with a one-track mind, and that she had lost her sense of humour. They made her sound like someone who was out to win the Teacher of the Year Award.

This rocked her and forced her into some honest self-appraisal. As she was a diary-writer, she wrote her responses to this eavesdropping, and she found that she filled three pages with explanations of why she was so obsessed with her career.

It brought about a radical change in her social self. She had at last taken time to counteract the formation of that one-sided person she was inevitably slipping into.

Summary

In this chapter, you have been asked to absorb the notion of a narratory. This is a feature of your self which is made by a whole range of factors in your life. But essentially, the most dominant influences which create this narratory are part of the accretions of everyday living, and you may find it difficult to distinguish the important from the small-scale ones. These are some main examples:

- Others' opinions
- Early assessments of you
- Your own valuation of your attainments
- Formal talk or writing about you
- Informal hearsay and conversation putting a value on you.

You have also noted the importance of understanding and applying a knowledge of the classical Greek concept of catharsis, and observed the importance of standing back to observe yourself as if from the outside. This distancing is valuable because it enables you to look afresh at acquired habits of mind.

Purposely writing down accounts of your nature and status with others is a powerful way to experience those insights into your deepest self which are so vital to you as a language –user, and language is the fundamental requisite of this effort towards revising and re-establishing your life with more meaning and spiritual well-being.

CHAPTER 4

Writing for well-being

It is time now to focus on the ways in which using and manipulating language can help in your general feeling of health and contentment. It has long been recognised that 'unloading' your troubles, as in the above discussion of catharsis, can help to counteract stress. But now we go deeper, into how words can positively enhance your sense of purpose and contact with the world. We also look at how the creative use of words can be used to re-evaluate and the entire nature of how individuals react to the world around them.

The nature of language is so important to your sense of being in the world, because it can go beyond simply defining things by giving basic facts. This book is about encouraging yourself to use language in the same artistic way that you might paint watercolour or write music. All this is fundamentally about your reasons for existing; about asserting your sense of self, whether or not you ultimately wish to write for others.

Words – giving therapy

Think about how and why children need to assign names to things. Calling a male person 'daddy' not only indicates a relationship and an identity of something other than themselves: it also makes them secure and describes their own position in their world. Words can suggest so much, and from a range of potential meanings we select all the time. Wars can start over the wrong use of words in diplomacy. There are thousands of active, purposeful ways to use language, but beginning with description is always useful in writing your new life.

It sounds so obvious, but consider what you do when you describe something. Description makes something fit into our scheme of meanings. As soon as we add adjectives like 'new' or 'period' to a description of a house, we suggest certain interpretations and dimensions. It is exactly the same with your life and how you write about it.

Memory capture

A powerful way to see this descriptive nature of words is to work on writing about a specific experience from your past. To do this, follow these steps in your journal:

1. Choose a photograph from the family album which includes you and a group of other people. Obvious

examples would be a celebration, a wedding or a reunion and so on. Study this and bring to mind the names, jobs, characters and voices of some of the others.

2. Now imagine what you might be thinking as you stand posing for the picture. Imagine you are thinking about these other people, or the event, or even the place itself. There is no need to write this down until stage three. For now, just project yourself into the scene.

3. Finally, turn the photograph over and write short notes: no more than a descriptive account to yourself. Try to put the life into the event by describing it as if you were a witness.

The same can be done with objects. You can choose an object which has personal significance, and write about a scene from the past in which that object was prominent.

Random responses

Now this can be developed. The act of writing from the notes will shape the people and events into a sequence. Concentrate on putting into words everything that was around you on that occasion.

Your descriptive passage, when you read it through, will have some or all of these features:
- Emotive language (e.g. I felt envious that time..)
- Words indicating your valuing of things (e.g. It upset me because…)
- Negative judgements (e.g. I felt that it achieved nothing.)
- Imaginings (e.g. The car reminded me of a space vehicle.)
- Factual data (His camera was a Pentax Spotmatic.)

For special notice are the words which highlight your own valuing – of others, of places, of experience. List the words which most signify your present judgement of the event. Even plain adjectives or words conveying causes of events may lead to more meaningful writing. You will need to keep revising thoughts and re-selecting particular words as you work.

An example

A photograph of children playing in a river – date 1941
Description:

Here, I was a child fishing for tiddlers. My friends and I all had nets we used to buy from the corner shop. Peter, the tall one, is dreaming as usual. Mary is peering at something in her hand. I think she caught a frog at one point. We were all so happy, as we were away from any kind of worry.

Who would guess that there was a war going on, and that the three children here are evacuees? Yes, I was a hundred miles from London where my family lived. I knew that bombs were probably falling on them, and that I would be safe. But it was not a happy time really: not when I made myself think about the troubles going on elsewhere. The best thing was the red-coloured stone I carried home.

Notice how this is mostly a case of giving the bare factual data, and yet it goes on to locate an emotional condition. Description can do this, and in doing so, it alleviates, releases captured feelings, and forces you to look again at experience. You could have done the same piece of writing for something that happened only a week or a month ago. It would be just as valuable.

Ideas- knowing the sanity of your imaginings
Of course, many of your thoughts about experience will involve dreams, fantasies and incredible ambitions. This is only natural, and is something that should be used daringly in these writing exercises. People indulge in imaginings all

the time, as in the middle-aged man who still dreams of playing football for his team at Wembley. But there is much value in placing yourself in a fantasy-identity in your writing. You might want to place a regular section in your journal in which you write about your other, imagined self: the one who took a different path earlier in life.

Your secondary self

A well-proven way to use this writing as a way to self-knowledge is to write an imaginary c.v. for the secondary you – the you who took a different route at a decisive point in your life. For instance:

1974   The real me took a course in French for Business. This helped to get my current secretarial post. Since that date I have done Computer literacy courses, had a family and joined a theatrical society to help satisfy my thespian interests.

1974   The secondary me went to drama school. I took my diploma, spent two years as a waitress, waiting for that big break. In 1977 I found an agent, and did some television advertising. My first real part was a small role in *Casualty*.

Note that the real purpose of this is to monitor the extent of your fantasies, and to enjoy the playfulness of this imagining – not to treat it as an exercise in detailing failure. A similar way to understand this is to ask a parent, or someone from an older generation, to summarise their lives, picking out decisive moments, and contrasting dreams with reality.

This exercise brings out the nature of your imposition of self on circumstances. To what extent have you allowed circumstances to rule your sense of your own worth and talent?

> *'Tis in ourselves that we are thus, or thus: our bodies are gardens, to the which our wills are gardeners.*
> Shakespeare, Othello

All this is not about negative feelings, however. As a writing exercise, it is really about being thankful for the achievements and sense of satisfaction your real self feels. In fact, there are dozens of reasons for our not having taken a certain path earlier in life. The writing here is aimed at describing the condition of your real self, and also in understanding the reasons for the imaginings.

Of course, as psychologists constantly tell us, without dreams and fantasies, we would be very ill. The release they give is more an outlet for a sense of play, of escape from the demands of routine. They are, much more importantly for the present purpose, the springboard of creative writing.

Imagine how much a successful writer needs the power of this imagining. The basis of writing is the art of extending reality into unreality, and this often accesses such experience as dreaming, as was the case with R.L. Stevenson's novel, *Dr.Jekyll and Mr. Hyde*: Stevenson first had the original idea for his story in a nightmare.

In your journaling, if you maintain some habit of writing about your imaginings, your extensions into unreal data, the rewards are rich and varied. If you ask a professional fiction-writer what the benefits of using the unreal, they might give some of these answers:

- It allows an escape from here and now
- It gives the reader and writer a new viewpoint on present shared reality
- It provides answers about the value of now
- It helps to put together the many-sided complexities of life

You can see from this that writing your imaginings is actually another strategy for understanding the real situation now: it puts into perspective all the unnamed frustrations and restlessness that emerge at times of stress or doubt, and helps you to clarify your aims.

Compiling a personal anthology

A valuable and rewarding part of your progress with language and with your emerging new self is the pre-writing activities you have indulged in. This involves looking at your favourite writing by others, and understanding what draws you to it. In the Elizabethan period, gentlemen kept 'commonplace books' in which they would write extracts and quotations from favourite authors. This idea could be extended into themes and subjects, very much as a writer keeps research records

Compiling a personal anthology is a neat way to register exactly what uses of words you personally admire most. This goes much further than simply assembling a 'Desert Island' Top Ten books. You should think about all the texts you have read – from the Bible to the latest thriller – and link them to subjects which particularly concern you.

Example

Imagine a journalist and writer who works freelance. She might have say four subjects which interest her: minorities in society; the history of race-relations; blues music and media representation of society. Although it would be easy to see and make links between all these, she might keep a cuttings file of writing about them, kept separately. Over a period of time, certain angles on the subject would begin to emerge. The writer would see a pattern, and this would reflect herself and her preoccupations.

You could do the same. Start by listing the subjects in life which constantly interest you. Note which sections of the daily newspaper you tend to read first. Which sections do you skip? Do you go straight to 'human interest' and skip the politics- and if so, why? From this, write a checklist of the top six subjects, then reflect on books, writers, poems, interviews – anything you have read that really sticks in the mind as something special.

There is no snobbery and elitism in this. Your selections could be Dickens or they could be from Catherine Cookson. The idea is to bring the passages to mind. If you can find the actual words, then copy them into a part of your journal labelled 'Personal anthology' arranged alphabetically. The thinking part of this is to concentrate on the passages or statements and determine their importance for you – for what you have developed as your point of view on the subject. Another benefit from this preparatory thinking is that when you progress to more extended passages of writing, you will more than likely write on a new aspect of one of this focal subjects.

Your access to your consciousness

A personal anthology is also a key to your most profound inter-relationships with the stuff of the world. In Vedanta Hinduism, there is a concept of *maya*. This refers to all the data and sensual stimuli of the world which impinge on your awareness, but which float by, never really being central to your self-understanding. To reject the distractions of *maya* is part of the way of Vedanta. For a writer, part of the climb towards this new life of sharpened awareness and focused direction is to turn away from things which are not significant to you.

Meditate on your personal anthology. Spend ten minutes before the active part of each writing session exploring the style and expression of the writing. Note how it differs from how you might express the same thought. It may be that it is simply the beauty of the sound-quality that attracts you, as in nonsense verse by Lewis Carroll. But nevertheless, there are deeper reasons why you are always drawn to that passage.

Learning from Patience/patients

An extension of this idea of going outside your own consciousness is the notion of empathy. Notice how writers have to write empathically, being sure they can create convincing fictional pictures of people very different from themselves (as in Shakespeare writing the part of Juliet, a fourteen-year-old girl).

An exciting way to start this is to recall the state of mind when you are ill and feel frustrated that you cannot operate in life as normal. Extend this into a more extreme example, and you have that aspect of writing that removes the focus from yourself. This is valuable, as it trains the mind to work with empathy, making you stretch yourself to imagine other states of being. A standard exercise in social care courses is for one student to put a cloth over her eyes and then to be guided, as if blind, by friends, around the college. Doing something akin to this is what provides the basis of empathic writing.

Reflections

1. As you sit down to write, bring to mind someone you have observed during the day: a stranger who leads a very different life to yourself.

2. Just free-flow write how you see them, do not judge them; react emotionally to them. An obvious example would be a street-beggar. But don't prescribe any rules about how you write, and include your personal/political opinions of begging in general if this happens. You are concerned here with one specific individual.

Listening to others' sub-texts

This is another productive strategy for stepping outside your own consciousness and learning about how you use language for healthy self-esteem. So many words are about opinion, judgement and more fundamentally – about people wanting to change the attitude and behaviour of others. Think about how others in your life seem to want to change you. Possibilities might be:

- Changing you so that you become comfortably summed-up
- Changing you for the 'better'
- Changing you so that you conform
- Changing you for 'your own sake'
- Changing you because they do not understand you

You could easily add to this list. But for the moment, spend some time listening to how other people in your life speak to you in terms of what you **do not do**. Or, how they speak about things you do that **they do not understand.** A large part of this talk might be around the way people circumscribe life: how they package it so that there is no part which cannot be explained.

Test responses by doing slightly unconventional things, or by purposely breaking routine. Even a simple thing such as starting a discussion on politics (if it is something you hardly ever do) might have a constructively unsettling outcome. Alternatively, you could look around shops and markets for a particular carving or model with symbolic significance; Eastern religions have plenty of these. Test others' reactions to your interest in collecting objects such as items from nature you might collect on a walk. Many writers collect stimulus objects and keep them on their desk to suggest images and close detail.

The interest here is in other people's responses The reactions to your increased awareness of the natural world or to wider religious and political belief will be catalysts to show changed behaviour in others. Some writers use different stones, grasses or butterflies to stimulate research and preparation for writing.

Their responses could be anything from incredulity to ridicule. But you will see the mechanisms of sub-texts in action. In other words, you will be judged, and others will try to fit the new aspect of your behaviour into how they want to see you. Now consider this same principle in relation to the more fundamental changes this course will cause in you.

Be prepared for the revolutions involved when you write and journal towards a more honest and courageous self. To put it simply: if you bring change into your own life with a sense of joy and innocence, then the writing will be enriched.

Notes

Write about six keywords which are used to define and explain you – by people who know you well (or so they think). Then write about these words as they cause reactions in you. Explain these reactions to yourself. For instance, you might be complimented because you always 'persevere'. What exactly is suggested to you by this word when pinned on you as a character-definition? Is it actually a compliment? Just write your feelings about each of these words.

When you have done this, follow it up by adding your own words which you would use to replace theirs. In comparing the two, you will be stepping closer to your own self-perception.

Case study

Sue never really knew how she felt about her husband's family's opinion of her. She wasn't sure whether it mattered. But there had always been a certain nameless unease when she was present at their family gatherings. She decided to log all the statements made about her, or put directly to her.

Over a period of several months, she noted and later wrote down these statements. Although on the surface the general view seemed to be that she was 'a good wife', this appeared to be defined by them as a woman who stayed at home, didn't expand her horizons and rarely complained. Sue decided that even her personal qualities such as creativity and courage (discussed at certain moments of crisis) had been shelved in order that a more familiar Sue was 'created' for the family archive, as it were.

By writing her reactions to several pages of comment about her, Sue assembled quite a detailed scenario in which she came across as more of a performer than as her genuine self. She was too concerned with these others and 'acted to their prescribed role'.

All this changed, guided by the passages of analysis in Sue's journal: here there was a living record of silent, unobserved pressure to conform. Her future course was one of quiet but definite subversion, so that her more authentic self could emerge into daily life.

Summary

In this chapter you have been asked to consider the power of words when placed as a valuing-agent on a person or on a particular experience. The ideas in here are about starting certain creative and analytical habits which are meant to deepen your reflections on how you are perceived – by yourself as well as by others around you.

We have seen that there are several dominant aspects of these potent words we all use to label and understand common experience:

- Words as instruments for empathy
- Words as explainers
- Words to define a feeling or a condition
- Loaded words, carrying valuing instruments
- Words which escape or avoid honesty.

Finally, you have been asked to experiment with some self-reflective strategies for preparing to write more profoundly and purposefully towards a clearer understanding of your aims, ambitions and most important of all, your creative centre of being. This creative centre will now be in focus.

CHAPTER 5

Life-scripts and adapting endings

The directions on the routes of this book so far have been towards a more honest and accurate understanding of the self. Regardless of what problems philosophy might have in defining what the 'self' actually is, we have to work with the idea that our self is a centre of feeling and thinking, something that needs the sustenance of imagination as well as security and familiarity.

But now you must turn attention to those forces in life which dictate the course your particular self should take. The journaling work will now face up to challenging that dynamic which makes you only a secondary self.

Not writing that obituary
On many rather glib self-development courses, and in business motivation seminars, there is one technique for reflection which has become a stock piece of the repertoire. This is the exercise where you are asked to write your own obituary. It is a chance to sort out those who want to aim at everything from those who want to achieve one specific condition. Of course, it also allows for people to note the

differentiation between those who want material success and powerful influence from those who simply want self-satisfaction.

Now is the time to ignore these superficial methods, in spite of the fun element, and confront your actual nature and function as determined by social forces. Read newspapers and watch current affairs programmes, and the word 'ideology' will constantly occur. Pundits will talk about how certain ideologies make us what we are, and that to be free we have to challenge them.

This chapter is about such challenges. It is about not being satisfied with a glib imagined obituary. The problem with the obituary is that it entices you to dream and to express certain wish-fulfilments. What should concern us even more urgently is what has made us the person we are now: at the starting-point of this writing course. Here are some possibilities.

Sources of your life-script
- How you were defined as a child
- Your own acceptance of certain roles
- Never being given the chance to question
- Being imprisoned in familiar routines
- Concentrating only on what is immediate

- Concentrating only on what is essential
- Ignoring the inner urgings for change

All these are extremely potent forces working on the individual. If you haven't done this before, then devote some thinking time to your 'created profile' now. How are you generally defined? Is it in terms simply of your profession or occupation? Do people stick labels like 'She's a nice girl' on you? Do the adjectives applied to you seem inappropriate?

A positive way to handle all these thoughts is to list all the aspects of your created profile. This profile is what has been made by broader social ideology and also by your peer-group and family.

A typical example of a created profile might be one made entirely of the surface others see. This might be caused by your conversation, your lack of any extreme behaviour, or even by your selections made to determine your wardrobe. If you have been wearing dark suits and conservative ties and shoes to work for several years, then one day you turn up wearing a yellow suit and a polkadot pink tie, then notions about you will change – but not how you want them, of course.

Think about your behaviour at a formal event such as a business meeting for instance. You might step into one of these roles:

Silent listener

Control freak

Monologue-speaker

Coffee-provider

Nodder and smiler

Deep and silent

And so on. In other words, a meeting is a useful metaphor for the ways in which the life-scripts are applied.

Who writes the script?

Also ask yourself which person or organisation is most responsible for making you he person you are? It could be your school, one individual, or the economic marketplace. But this life-script is grinding away, generating new words for you to keep on creating the same script dialogue every day. It is a kind of programming, and you need to break out.

My life-script has made this created profile:

Childhood: +   sociable/ funny/ good company/ invite her to a party.

	−	won't speak her mind. Never talks about serious things
	−	One-sided. What you see is what you get.
Youth:	+	Knowledgeable about films and music.
	+	Likes to talk about television but not relationships
	−	Good company, if you like stones
	−	Listens – rarely leads.
Adult (now!)	+	Solid, dependable, nothing striking.
	+	Bland, middle-of-the –road
	−	Fair-weather friend. Can drift into own concerns
	−	Too aloof. In a world of her own.

Fig. 2. Created Profile

This gradual laying-down of a created profile makes simply a superficial you. It is superficial largely because you do not actively alter it, deepen it, by making your social self an identity which is close to the inner self. In other words, you need a way to make the sense of being in the world more honest and more clearly defined.

The life-script, largely written by others but affirmed by yourself – usually without thinking – may have been established in such a way that large portions of what you sense inside you have been missed out. This, again, is what creative writers often access in their imagination: the nature of the self in them which has never been known.

It is as if we all have a dark cellar down inside us, and we are the only ones with the right torch to shine into it. So how do we put that torch into others people's hands?

Writing from the affirmatives

One thing that can be done is to write about these unknown areas inside you. In your journal, try this exercise to access the hidden creative self beyond the secondary one. Choose something that you rely on –something crucial to your own life and self-esteem. It might be a musical instrument, or even some jewellery. It might be a part of your body you rely on for work, or even a car or a computer. Think about what this means to you, and prepare to describe it as if in praise.

Random responses

The category of the object chosen may be concrete or abstract:

Concrete: a pen, a hammer, a car etc.

Abstract: brain, love, trust, independence etc.

Write notes in praise and gratitude to this, explaining why it is so central in your life. Imagine how important a tent is to a Mongolian tribesman in the desert, or how crucial a cow is to a Masai in Kenya. Place your object or quality in that category of importance.

Now, ask yourself how many other people know this about you and how you feel about it? Often, this exercise makes us aware of the extent to which we never reinforce our identity with others – as we often consider things beyond explanation, or even not worth talking about at all.

Example

You might only have thought of your car – the car you rely on to commute to work most days of the week. It might seem odd, but your reliance on that car exists as a bond of dependency, just as the Mongolian with his tent. His loving care of the sewing of the tent is part of a contract in a way.

You and your car might be the same. You might give your car a nickname, or even talk to it as if it were alive! The point is, your words of admiration reflect something deep in you – and something creative. Look at the words you used in description of it. One person might think of a car as simply 'something to get me from a to b' while another might actually have a passionate interest in design and aesthetic appearance.

This is all related to those almost numberless affirmative elements in ordinary life which tend to be ignored because of some grand game-plan called 'career': these might be anything from simple pleasures to massive unsung achievements and personal qualities such as

- Skills with making things: DIY
- Ability to share a child's imaginative life
- Patience looking after someone who is ill
- Helping older people cope with everyday things
- Writing a newsletter for a club or society
- Cycling to work as your part in Green politics

All these activities involve you and a particular possession – a skill, a machine, a personal quality and so on – and maybe all unknown to several people simply because you never talk about it. This is not to say that bragging is essential. It is sharing that is under discussion. The case of the daughter who could not ask for help sums it up. This girl needed some of her mother's time to help with her study as a mature student. She was not too proud to ask, but too considerate. She thought that her mother placed no value on education and felt that it would not be a valid reason for which to ask for help. In the end, she had to stop her studies. Then she found out that her mother had been looking at brochures about advanced study with her daughter in mind!

It was simply a mental construct in the daughter's mind which had been formed by her inferring things from her mother's small talk.

Making the little universe spin

The result of this is that there is a need to be aware of how important our own initiative is. We are largely responsible for sustaining this creative centre which makes the torch shine in the blackness of our depth and complexity. If you are trapped in an ideology of consumerism for instance, where you sense that everything around you runs counter to your sense of self as an independent spirit, you will feel this unease even when you buy ready-meals for the microwave at a supermarket. There will be a feeling of dull conformity if you have seen yourself as an individual. The script can be re-written.

> *We can play the same part so many times that the mask or pretence begins to slip. The words are dead; we don't believe them any more. But there is only one author and only one script, unless we turn playwright.*

So how do you make that little universe of you start spinning on its own, without being reliant on the greater cosmos, where everything turns together at the same speed?

Reflections

One potential route to success here is to actually dramatise a scene in which the real self is the main character. Write this as a telephone conversation between the self of the created profile and the deeper self wanting to be realised. Part of your role as a journaler is to write in experimental ways and break the moulds which may restrict you to a one-dimensional view or yourself. The rationale behind this is to stand back and be the other, in order to understand better the existing attitudes applied to you by others.

What and why you love

Eventually, all these reflections lead to questions of emotional being, of course. This is because so many of the elements that make up the deeper self are only important to us, and they exist because we do not question them: they are simply spontaneous, and in truth they are integral to our sense of self. Why would someone want to start learning to play the piano at the age of fifty? People do, and they cannot often offer more explanation than 'It's something I've always wanted to do.' The obvious conclusion is that it is some calling of the spirit at last fulfilled.

For these reasons, you have to start writing about what you love and why you love, and you need to do it now. Time has a habit of beating away all your plans and schedules. Better to write free-flow now about these determining features of yourself. These are questions of affiliation, trust, dependence, need, giving and so many other things which have been the themes of great writing and art.

As an illustration, think about the elements in your relationships that are part of a 'chalk and cheese' idea. What people are you drawn to just because they are different from you? A good starting –point for exploring your loving nature is to consider how you approach the idea of opposition. For instance, why do you put up with another person's ways of living when they are so unlike yours? Which words would you use to explain your reasons?

Sacrifice

Tolerance

Pity

Understanding

Neglect

Curiosity

Anything for a quiet life

Fascination

It's interesting that this list highlights some elements which may not appear to have anything at all to do with the nature of 'love' as commonly understood. For instance, to write about 'pity' in an account of love may seem strange, but it may be that pity is a substitute for love in some cases, and in others, totally a version of love. Charity is a kind of love, and may be generated simply through pity.

Notes

Exploring the nature of your loving and your experience of love will lead to other massive subjects, so start small. Start with description again, and take the famous poem by

Rupert Brooke as your model. His poem 'The Great Lover' beginning 'These things I have loved' can be adapted to:

The..........Lover   (put in your own adjective)

First line: *These things I have loved/* or *This is how I love*

Then list your answers

Spinning epics of success

The point of this development into scripting your own life is to think on a large scale. Move away from the small-scale domestic frames of living that hem you in. If you think about it, this inner you we have isolated is a massive unknown area, mainly because we spend most of life just being rather than reflecting on being. Your new writing habits will change all this, but you have to think in terms of an epic.

An epic is a story about a triumph in adversity and a quest to find something with huge consequences for the hero. It might be acceptance, or victory over adversity. In your case, it could be no more than an insight into your condition through hard work or hard thinking but it is just as significant. An epic usually has grand, stylish language in the telling, and that is the point here.

We introduce here the need to be poetic, to express the matters of the spirit, of the normally inexpressible. A useful first step here is to articulate what the end of your quest might be.

So, what is it you want from life? In your journal so far you have explored a whole range of aspects of your sense of sense and your sense of being someone with peers and relationships. Now we have turned the attention to yourself as a character with a script, and a chance to write a new script. Everyone reading a story starts to anticipate the end, the closure.

By indirections we directions find

This statement was made by Polonius, in Shakespeare's *Hamlet*. He was hinting that we often find answers by accident or without too open a design or plan. Your journaling should be the same. Purposes will emerge. You don't need to state that massive game-plan and you can keep the objectives and personal goals quite obscure until they emerge naturally. If any have emerged, then monitor them.

An example might be: you could have realised in the course of writing that you spend too much time 'revisiting' the past and that you feel that this is unhealthy. But the more you write and think, the more you feel a sense of discovery, as if you are searching for something you know by instinct to be important for you. Well, by all means rethink, and try to express the new insight. It may be that your preoccupation with the past is a way of answering questions about now. A familiar example is when we compare our personalities to our parents and feel a sense of similarity in more than a vague physical resemblance.

Your struggle for certainty and self-knowledge is an epic for you because:
- It involves startling honesty and directness
- It is loaded with opposition
- Others may discourage you
- The quest is against familiarity and comfort
- It involves language you normally avoid (e.g. poetic vocabulary)

But never forget that the poetry is essential. In your writing, always accept a powerful metaphor if your unconsciousness suggests it to you – rather than a plain statement of literal fact. For instance, you might meditate on a sentence such as 'My life now seems like a river full of rapids and I'm looking for a dependable canoe.' The poetic interest is in the personal truth of how you perceive the life-challenge. That is, you are clearly now seeing life as a struggle, but the river may also be irresistably attractive: far more so than a straight road in a comfortable car.

Case study

Simon had been on numerable business seminars and his life in junior management was beginning to feel nothing more than hollow words and plans for the future. He felt as though each day was making his sense of purpose in life recede, merely because there was never a sense of achievement: only a sense of planning achievement. It was when reading a magazine left in the office that he came across an interview with a writer who talked about keeping a diary of story ideas. The writer used to imagine himself as others and write in the first person, usually in some exotic, wealthy holiday-spot.

Simon knew that he often dreamed of other places and of being another person – the person he had imagined for himself at school when he dreamed of owning a communications business. He realised that his plans to work for himself rather than for another had been shelved.

He wrote about his past, regularly in a diary, and worked back to revisiting that earlier version of himself who had planned to be a 'tycoon.' What Simon discovered was not a business plan but a state of being, and imaginative excitement which he had lost. He realised that writing in detail about this earlier self made its recreation seem more attainable. It was a launch-pad for replenishing his energy, his sense of realising a passionate youthful ideal.

He knew that it was not going to be easy, but at least his writing had reminded him of the right path and he felt that retracing his steps and starting again would not be absolutely impossible.

Summary

In this chapter you have been asked to consider and write about the power to imagine another version of yourself- a successful, fulfilled version which reaches into a self with a life-script written by you rather than by others. We have seen that this involves;

- Being honest about your perceptions of yourself in society
- Understanding others' influences on your life
- Thinking frankly about your emotional being
- Putting into words the previously inexpressible

The development into writing imaginatively about your deepest sense of self touches on poetic, philosophical material; but finally, it is about finding the right words to reveal what you know to be important and essential for you, rather than accepting what routine, career, relationships and family might load upon you.

CHAPTER 6

The Docudrama of Your Present

You are now at a point at which everything is ready and in place for you to look at your situation afresh. The last chapter was about changing the life-script, and now we follow that image further by thinking of each individual life as a drama – as in the television 'docudrama' in which real life is made dramatic, sometimes authentic and at other times with a 'stagey' feel as if the reality turned into acting for the camera.

This chapter is all about that odd, bizarre but amazingly creative clash inside you: the one that mixes what you feel is authentic to you and the sheer performance for others.

In this clash lies a deep source of writing and self-knowledge.

Looking from the outside in

As Robert Burns said, we need the 'giftie' to 'see ourselves as others see us.' But the point made there can be taken further. Notice that when you try to stand back and see your values, your communication and your emotional and intellectual expression, the prison of routine has a habit of blocking the view. For this reason, you need some writing strategies to clear the view. The basis of this is meditation and reflection on what you think about the notion of judging yourself by *having* or *being*.

In eastern religions, great emphasis is often placed on *being*, of course, and eastern art often simply describes, rather than analyses or seeks for reasons for being.

To have or to be

You must have thought about how much a consumer society mediates the idea of defining the individual by what he or she possesses. The message seems to be that you are worth consideration if your car or your computer or even your mobile phone is the 'state of the art' version. There is also a strong tendency to judge success by age and appearance. On a recent documentary about aspiring novelists, one literary agent openly confessed this a publisher would have offered a smaller amount of money if his writer-client had been older, despite the writing being just as impressive. So how do you value identity – are you influenced by this culture of aspiration?

What you should do is dwell on what you have: even if that is simplicity, very ordinary and not at all ultra modern.

Start by listing what you have and what you do in a ranked list of personal importance. For example:

<u>John Smith:</u>

I have –

A wife and two children

A semi-detached house with three bedrooms

A Ford Focus

A job in advertising…….. etc.

I do-

Show my love for my family

Country walks

Keep a collection of coins

Play squash

Take part in conversations in the pub

Notice how difficult it is to place certain items at the top. People come first of course, but then how do you assess the worth of very simple things such as talking to your partner or keeping in touch with friends? The only way to develop a real sense of value here is to stop and place value on what you have and do.

Random responses

For this writing exercise, you are to prepare by taking your notebook with you on a tour of the house. The idea is that you look closely at each room, register the things concerned with each room that you really value and that you are thankful for. The piece of writing you are planning is a *gratitude statement*.

For instance, the tour of the house might include these thoughts:

- The photographs of my son as a child
- That cup he won for football
- My work decorating our bedroom
- Making that desk in the office
- The holiday in Spain – remembered by seeing the map.
- The security of this home
- The warmth we make in the living-room (human warmth!)

The writing emerging from this has to do with purposely meditating on the aspects of the life you have made for you and for those you love. The human living-together reflected in your home is what counts. This is about something you have which is not marketable, of course. There is no market value for the feelings of attachment to your partner or family.

You might include an account of what your *being* is about – as opposed to your having. A list of points here might include some statements about *how you exist*.

1. I exist as a creature who loves and values
2. I exist as a supportive person
3. I exist as someone coping with many roles in life
4. I exist as a thinking being who knows the past
5. I exist as someone who enjoys this moment now

The list could go on. The basic idea is to write with gratitude for these blessings – anything from skills you have to your deep presence in others' lives. Give thanks in this writing to the power of the simple things in what is usually so mundane that you pass it by without a thought.

> *'Men work together'* I told him from the heart,
> *'Whether they work together or apart.'*
> Robert Frost: 'A Tuft of Flowers'

Your Creative p.o.v. explained

You are at the centre of so many varieties of interplay every day that it can be perplexing and confusing, trying to understand how you fit in. Just consider the roles you play with each person you meet on an ordinary basis. You are in fact the centre of this docudrama and you need to learn how to act but also how to come out of the part you play. This is where your creativity is essential. Creativity is made from:

- A sense of play
- A need to escape
- A longing for pretend alternatives
- A need to solve a problem
- A drive to make new

Right at the heart of this is your creative p.o.v. This is point of view – but in the sense used by a film-maker it is all related to how a story is seen by others, and how a p.o.v. gives a certain bias to the events told. In your creativity, there is such a p.o.v. Imagine that you have a camera in you, that you see life as a camera sees it, differing with the amount of light, the angle of the shot, the movement in the shot and so on. Each of us has this camera-view and we can use it as creatively as the best director.

For example, imagine that with a simple piece of camera-work you can shift your self-knowledge, just as a camera can shoot through a keyhole rather than straight at a face approaching a door. Do the same for yourself. It is all a matter of 'watching yourself' and then bringing in some changes. Imagine this camera follows you doing a sequence of things, almost as a storyboard. These might be the shots:

1. Having coffee thinking about which option to take from all the jobs in line that morning.
2. Checking the cupboard for cleaning equipment.
3. Phone rings. A friend wants to call round.
4. You tidy the lounge.
5. She hasn't arrived yet. You start writing a letter.
6. Friend arrives – you welcome her and start chatting

This contains no inner tensions, no conflicts, no expression of what your mind is actually doing. The frustrations of not doing the chore are counterbalanced against spending quality time with a friend. The creative p.o.v. here is to monitor the frustration but also the friendship. If it was a docudrama from your life, the storyline would be about this dilemma. Which does your camera see well and which does it distort?

This all depends on what is in your camera – what film, if you like. Ask yourself what is already inside, running on that loop, always coming around every day, as part of how and what you see. Then change the film – and change the camera-shots.

Handling the camera-work

A camera sees things flat and direct from your normal p.o.v. Now it's time to break this. An example would be this:

Subject:	Mrs. Jones, a 70-year-old neighbour you see and chat to every day. You talk about the weather and the price of milk.
Your p.o.v.:	She is a nice face, a pleasant smile. But basically she delays you as you Want to get the shopping done, or go to the dentist by 10.30.
Shot-change:	Extreme close-up. For God's sake, have a proper conversation. Make Time. She has her story, and will enrich yours. Write/rewrite her story In terms of the facts and in your reaction to them.

Remember that this works in reverse. Everyone you meet daily has this one main shot of you in their mind. Change their p.o.v. also. Do different things; set up unusual responses. In the consequences of this lies your creative centre. This is not to suggest eccentricity or sheer attention-seeking. It can be a very trivial thing such as asking about where someone was born or what stage they are at in their evening class.

Writing and self-knowledge have a basis in that special variety of creative thought which comes from imagining other lives, but it is not written in gold anywhere that we have to invent 'characters' in order to understand humanity. Every house and street is rich with human experience and untold stories.

Textless history

Spend some time assessing just how much of an average human life is unknown, unrecorded, and totally anonymous. Reflection on the absolutely minute status of an anonymous individual should encourage the imaginative use of every second. This is because only by maximising your own valuable time will your quality of being rather than having be recognised.

If we valued each life simply by what the person owned or achieved in public life, it would be a sad reflection on our interest in the fundamental mystery of being. As a writer, you have to access that dark, unexplored selfhood and only by creative camera-work in language will that be achieved. There are ways of putting texts into this potentially textless history.

- Write about the apparently trivial as if it were of major significance.
- Record your passing interpretations of the data of life
- Assess how and what you share with others
- Compare your desires for solitude and privacy with others
- Use words as hooks into other perspectives

Reflections

Now it is time to bring these thoughts together into a journaling exercise. You are going to write about one specific experience as if it were a scene in a film. For example, here is a scene from the life of Anonymous:

Scene 1 Interior. Day.
The study.
Pete, a novelist, is scribbling down ideas for the next chapter. So far, six have failed and we see the hand throwing paper into a bin.
Pete (inner thoughts): It's always the same – I try to write about my dad and the words all go dead. I try to catch his voice and it all sounds just like any guy on any street...

Pete frowns. Stands up, walks to stare out of the window
Voice over: Father's voice in Pete's head:
Son, you don't kick the ball like that, with your damned toe-end. See, watch me, here... see the way?

This technique is a rough version of a filmscript. You can find any example of layout in any handbook on screenwriting. The important point is that you *dramatise yourself*, standing back, looking from the outside. Just by making the effort to do this, you will highlight something fresh about yourself.

Bringing in the creative scriptwriter

How can you find ways of writing like this, accessing this scriptwriter in you? There are several possibilities, but a useful one is to discover aspects of yourself by using objects – everyday items in your life. For instance, here is the key-ring stimulus exercise:

Stage One.

Take your key-ring and note all the different uses of the keys. Think of the things they open. For example, you might have (a) a key for your front door (b) a suitcase (c) a shed (d) a personal diary (e) a briefcase

Stage two

Write some notes on each one – on what exactly it gives access to. Your front door is not only access to a hallway and a dining room. It opens up security, comfort, a 'nest', a place of love and so on. Do this for every key.

Stage three

Use the idea of a key in as many ways as possible. Brainstorm the word and think of as many ideas about keys as possible. Here is a list to help you start:

A key to a heart

The key to a problem

A key format

Secret key

Keycode

In your list you will find some imagistic uses that will apply to your locks and doors.

Researching the audience of one

Surely by now you have realised what a puzzle you are. A human is a bundle of complexity and contradiction. In yourself, however, that little universe discussed earlier is now increasingly seen as a dark, shadowed, unknown world. You only see a tiny proportion of your being and potential being each moment.

How can writing reveal this audience of one – the self who listens to the self in that everyday monologue of our stream of consciousness? There are some well-established methods. Here are some of the main ones, and you can use one of these in your last writing exercise for this chapter:

1. The waste-bin exercise

Think about the contents of your waste-bin. What do these reflect about you? The categories of food, cosmetics, stationery, clothes, packaging etc. all form a picture of a lifestyle.

2. Photo-sequence

Extract a collection of photographs of yourself from the family records and put these images in a line. Note and log the changes, and the main features of your appearance at each stage in your life.

3. Your ideal room

Write an account of the ten gadgets you could not do without in your ideal room. These can be a mix of work and play items, and can even include toys and games. Then write about why you chose these and what it says about your current situation.

4. Holiday preferences:

Think of a typical holiday spent with others. What would be your favourite ways of spending your time, regardless of whether these are group activities or things you wish to do alone. Then write notes on your reasons for these activities.

Notes

For this exercise, then, choose one of the above options and now, write from another viewpoint. That is, write in the third person- he/she – and tell the events or characteristics you have listed above. The purpose of this is to reveal certain features of yourself that would not normally be apparent. Most of this chapter has been about the lost self – the submerged part of you which is never fully explained to anyone or known by your conscious mind. This writing piece is intended to describe something fundamental simply by logging behaviour. Often this pinpoints your choices from a range of options and why you tend to choose certain things. For instance, the exercise might show why you tend to choose the 'easy option' and do anything for a quiet life. Maybe you want to change this? Your docudrama may be becoming a little stale and predictable.

Again, simply write from the lists, without using your brain – concentrate on instinctive responses, and describe rather than analyse.

Case Study

Sue felt as though her life was just a film with two locations: office and flat. She lived with two other girls who worked in the city, and they had intended to go out and meet people, living a happy and busy single life. But work changed all that. Sue found herself taking work home every night, and the reason for this was usually that she had no enthusiasm for the tasks in the day, and postponed as many as possible, spending time on trivia or on long conversations with her colleagues. Then by five o'clock there was a lot to take home.

She knew instinctively what the problem was, but had not stopped to work it out and try to change it. When a description of this behaviour in her journal was written, it led to a conversation with her flatmates. They had noticed that she rarely went out for a drink with them any more, but had assumed it was the demands of her career.

In her journal, Sue described a typical hour of her day in the office. She found that a massive amount of time was spent I unnecessary e-mails and telephone conversations simply because the sight of her files waiting attention on the desk was depressing. She was using avoidance tactics but not solving the discontent.

She read over her words and then talked it all through. Somehow, through habit, she had lost sight of why she had ever started her career in the first place. The journaling had acted as a 'staff appraisal' exercise but by herself for herself! It brought about a re-think.

Summary

In this chapter, you have been asked to think of your life in terms of the metaphor of a drama. The advantage of this line of approach to change is that it initiates a re-think about yourself. But it also has certain aspects of making space for some genuine thinking and reflection. These are its outstanding advantages:

- It is a metaphor meant to highlight your sense of self
- In ordinary experience, we miss the simple joys and values
- It is a way of valuing being over having
- We are complex creatures who ignore the obvious and seek complexity

In addition, we have looked at several writing methods of accessing your inner feelings, and describing the deeper condition of self which normally lie dormant in a working day. You have been asked to look again at the patterns of normality and see how a creative use of language may regenerate your condition as a public and private person. The writing exercises throughout the chapter have been designed to pinpoint this range of potential shortcomings in the way we see and judge our public self, distinguishing between private and performing self.

In the end, you are your own audience. Write for your self, as if from the outside, describe typical behaviour and then look for the significance. It has also reinforced a basic idea of this book: escape the claustrophobia of only ever looking at your life from the familiar viewpoint.

CHAPTER 7

Sharpening Skills of Self-Development

Now it's time to turn some attention to the most workable and practical way to ensure that your thinking and writing time is always related to a base of selfhood. Everything so far has been about looking at yourself from outside. Have you ever stopped to consider what is going on inside – in what the poet, W.B.Yeats said was 'the foul rag and bone shop of the heart'? What he meant by that is that a writer and creative person should never be afraid to look honestly into their emotional framework. One way of doing this is in a conventional sense is to attend a writing workshop.

But the assumption here is that you are working alone, with meditation time, private time. In that case, I have adapted the workshop idea to meet a quiet, reflective time, singular, not plural.

Introducing workshops
What is a workshop? There has been a proliferation of creative workshops in recent years, and in the case of creative writing, the typical workshop session is one in which a group of people work to a theme or subject, often

with stimulus material provided by a tutor or leader (sometimes a professional writer) and everyone works to a set method or stylistic direction. Usually, work is read aloud or circulated for objective comment. The workshop is usually for writers aspiring to have their work published.

The benefits are wide-ranging:

- Feedback on your work
- Meeting other writers
- Learning about working methods
- Having a chance to ask questions
- To relate your approach to others' writing
- Having the time and space to focus on writing

You might wonder how this could be related or adapted to someone working on his or her own? The idea of freedom to write and space to write is at the core of the idea, so there is no reason to define a workshop as merely a group activity, at least in principle. For instance, solitude can add something extra.

The power of solitude

It has been well established by psychologists and critics that several cases of notable creative minds were indeed so because of their need for solitude. The Romantic image of the lonely artist communing with nature perhaps expresses this in a distorted way, something of a stereotype, but essentially, you make your own solitude.

Being alone means that your mind is in a receptive condition. It will roam at random to find topics that match your mood. When you try to discipline this towards a goal, as in meditation, you are beginning that shaping process that leads to writing structures. For instance, dealing with silence and with solitude is not the same thing. But you can exploit them in a similar way. Both are valuable now, and very rare in modern life. They each, in a different way, open up possibilities. The way to start is with a development of the ordinary object and what it suggests. For example, you might, while sitting alone in your room, really observe a chair. Look at a chair in such a way that you let your mind develop connections.

Psychologists are now certain that solitude is attractive to the creative personality because it opens up the imagination by means of a latent, receptive space in which ideas can penetrate. It is almost as if solitude, even when in its noisy form, is an experience deliberately sought out in order that the greatest potential for creativity might be opened up. There is a scene in the film *New York Stories*, in which Nick Nolte (playing a visual artist) works frantically to the point of exhaustion on a huge mural, to the accompaniment of loud rock music. The ghetto-blaster is marked with paint from his hands. The artist needs noisy solitude, even to the point of excluding every other stimulus in life. So both noise and silence clearly have their place in the creative temperament and its workings.

The Chair

Shape? Material? Size? How is it classified?

Different perspectives: How would a carpenter see a chair? Perhaps he would be dismantling it mentally, thinking about the joints and technical abilities reflected in its manufacture.

Uses? Human connections?   Who might have sat in it? A Victorian rocker for instance – a woman with a small child, or an old man who has finished his working life in the mill? Metaphorical dimension: A chair is a support, a comfort? Are people potentially like chairs – to other people in need? Why kind of chair would such a person be?   Solid, accommodating, very formal, well-worn and homely? Office chair?

This list could go on for a long time, but it is an instance of how in the space of solitude, you can explore possibilities until you find a writing theme which applies to you more deeply than in your everyday consciousness.

Solitude has this tremendous potential to ask the mind to fill a vacancy. Clear your mind of the trappings of the day when you accept quietness and isolation. Shut out distractions.

Notes

Try your own version of the above expansion of an object. Use the headings and questions about the object as above, and this will lead to a piece of personal writing. Write as if it is simply a meditation at first. The shaping can come later.

Other potentially fascinating examples might be a pen, a letter, a typewriter, a garden tool or a dress.

Solitude also implies the time and space for a personally-generated silence. Even if there is noise just a few rooms or yards away, you can still create a silence in your spirit. Actually being still, in every sense, opens up our sense of wonder. Make for yourself a ritual each time you start a 'workshop of one' like this:

- Keep special objects in prominent places – perhaps a photograph or a paperweight.

2. Always have your pen or pencil in a place to hand, ready and comfortable
3. Surround yourself with gentle, calming supportive aids to creativity: things with colour or shape. Some writers hold a stone, or focus on a candle-light.
4. Do the small rituals in a significant order.

> *What is this life, if full of care,*
> *We have no time to stand and stare?*
> W H Davies

Doing the Workshop of One Routine

In a group workshop, the objective of presenting members with a stimulus is at the core. The tutor has to provide something that will present a 'point of entry' into a private world of imagery and autobiography. Therefore, universal stimuli are often used. Elemental substances, feelings, possessions, views: these are the commonest stimuli. The workshop of one routine means encouraging this process for yourself.

First, think about how the idea of joy and wonder are common to us all – maybe most often in childhood – but nevertheless, all human beings know the sheer inexpressible feeling of an epiphany, a revelation of some kind of 'truth'. Marghanita Laski called these experiences 'ordinary ecstasy' and by this she meant the fleeting sense of insight and understanding we feel at particular moments.

You can use this idea to study an example of a process of writing at your 'workshop of one':

Stage one:

Bring to mind a time when you experienced a moment of insight, such as looking at a baby being fed, or two children walking arm in arm, or maybe just a twilight scene over the ocean.

Stage two:

Write an account of that scene as if it were a photograph in front of you. Concentrate on visual detail.

Stage three:

List the sensual data as you recall them, as a witness: smell, touch, taste, sound. You might remember a boat on the water. What was the sound of the water? Did you pick up an oar, or a wet rope? How did it feel?

This assembles a sense of that re-created wonder. Wonder is, of course, killed by facts. But this does not mean that science has to be the enemy here. Quite the opposite is the case. Your moment of insight might involve staring at the vastness of space and the fear instilled by thoughts of infinity. As the French philosopher, Pascal, said, 'The silence of this infinite space terrifies me.' But that terror can be thought about, comprehended, and turned into creative vocabulary.

So the workshop of one involves these three elements:

1. The ritual, setting up the right atmosphere, inviting imaginative feeling.
2. The stimulus object
3. Your meditation on that object.
4. Writing a pen-sketch of what is recalled.
5. Developing this into a structured piece.

Planning your workshops

You can actually design a pattern of topics, all organically related. If you know that there is one area of your life and self that you wish to explore for several sessions, then list the conflicts, tensions and opposites in this topic, and make each one a workshop focus. You might want to deal with a certain insecurity, for instance, such as fear of failure, or a feeling that you are not accepted by others in a specific context.

A fruitful first step is to make the most of your attitudes to solitude. This is important because there is a profound relationship between solitude and the idea of the self, of individualism. It makes sense to plan your individual workshops around the need for solitude in your life, as opposed to your need to be in groups, to find solidarity with your neighbours and so on. As Thomas de Quincey said, 'No man ever will unfold the capacities of his own intellect who does not at least checker his life with solitude'.

I would like to introduce at this point the idea that there is much to learn from the therapeutic uses of this solitary self-knowledge. Anthony Storr has argued that there are two factors which promote recovery: making a plan or pattern out of his distress in order to make sense of it, and making a positive relationship with someone else. (See Storr's book, Solitude (details in the bibliography).

Plan your workshops of one with this in mind. This is an example of the pattern a typical workshop might have:
1. List the benefits you feel you derive from being alone and from being with others.
2. Think about examples of language associated with solitude and how they might apply to you. You might choose prayer, meditation, plea for help, praise for the good things, confessional words and other types of expression.

3. Relate something from list one with one of the subjects from list two. You might link a religious sense, a sense of wonder, with praise for good things. This would give rise to a workshop on *gratitude*.

   Taking gratitude as a subject opens up a whole range of possibilities. Consider what elements of your life are important but rarely fully acknowledged. If you can choose some of these, then you are prepared for the actual journal exercise which is the next step.

Random responses

For your journaling now, you are to use a preparation exercise called *the experience of possession*. This is a writing passage based on gratitude. The idea is that you take a notebook and walk from room to room in your home, as you did in the previous chapter. But this time you are considering only your prized possessions. Think about the idea of transience, as in the Biblical story about the rich man entering Heaven through the eye of a needle. The idea behind that is simply the notion of wealth being an encumbrance, and the suggestion here is that the Latin word for wealth and possessions, *impedimenta*, suggests a rather Puritan way of looking at possessions.

Turn this idea round and recall all the reasons why you came to own these treasured objects. Every one will have a story behind it. As you note down these things, bear these points in mind:

- In what place or setting you acquired it.
- Note the memory link to an experience in your past
- A simple possession that you think is beautiful
- The human presence in the thing – maybe objects made with skill.
- The shape, view, texture – all aspects of the object's attraction...

The aim here is to stop and meditate on the familiar. If you think about it, a possession is very much a reflection of personality and taste. You only have to note the obvious example of a wedding gift. It is easy to see the symbols and trappings of a formative period in a life: the thinking behind the gift, the traditional nature as opposed to the personal significance, the style items all give away something about aspiration and fundamental nature. Apply the same idea to a piece of special interest such as a ring, an item of clothing or a book.

When you are back from your mental journey, choose one object and write your journal entry on that one thing.

Amplify the notes into a piece of writing about gratitude. What are you thankful for? It could be a major concern like the fact that your possession marks a special friendship; that a thing always had happy associations in it, or even a small note such as 'this is the pen given to me by my aunt Julie when I passed my exams.' Any of this may give rise to some searching, revelatory writing.

The gratitude element here is part of a larger phenomenon, and one that is becoming increasingly important in today's world in which such a small amount of time is given to dwelling on significance. In a way, this is like the simple rituals suggested in habits like afternoon tea. In taking time to drink tea, to be sociable and enjoy the occasion, we are giving gratitude for friendship and the simple joys in life. Treat your time for possessions in a similar way. Maybe some of them are made to be used, and you have neglected that use. An example would be a walking stick or a hat for fell-walking – something you used to do ten years ago but now you never make time for. Do you actually regret not making time for that?

Gratitude is very much about celebrating your choices in life. You have chosen to take certain options, and your everyday objects are testimonies to those few choices from the infinite number of choices which life has to offer.

Taking time for the object tour, like the house tour, forces you to rethink your priorities. A typical example would be a musical instrument. A friend of mine always wanted to play guitar. At school, he never had music lessons. Then, at the age of forty, he finally bought an acoustic guitar and vowed to learn how to play it. More years passed. All he did was occasionally pick it up from its neglected place propped in the corner of his study. More time passed. Finally, he had a few weeks away from work and booked himself a place in an evening class. After six weeks he had learned how to play Bobby Shaftoe and smiled with delight like a child.

That guitar had always had an attractive quality for him. He would pick it up, loving the feel and the shape of it, adoring the sounds as he brushed the strings. Even without its music, it was a thing to celebrate and to love. Your possessions will have qualities like that. Gratitude therefore rejoices in that choice you made. It also marks the richness of life: its plenitude and what it offers freely. 'The best things in life are free' maybe a contentious statement for some, but it is difficult to deny the contrast between the expensive material possessions given to us and the 'gifts' of nature such as a surprise rainbow or a wonderful sunset.

This journaling exercise can therefore be extended into any exploration of gratitude you wish. Some commonly used aspects of the whole subject are these:

- Friends and the nature of your friendships
- Objects which have special importance for you – however trivial
- The contrast between the objects you possess and those you had in the past
- Things you use and rely on – 'friends' in that sense.

Sharing your workshops

Again, it might seem strange to mention this in the context of journaling, but now is the time to consider working with someone else on a collaborative piece of writing. But that someone may in fact not be present, or indeed, alive! By this I mean, a workshop with a group often includes a stock of stimulus objects. Start to assemble your own, and maybe a productive way to start this is to collect a set or display for your desk based on another person who is, or has been, close to you. For instance:

Stimulus objects

Person: Your father.

Example: Your father's autograph book.

Development: Add to this central focus object a group of small items – such as a photograph, birth certificate, a screwdriver used by him, a hat, a music cassette and so on.

Key image: Now work out something that would be representative of the man you knew. What one event or aspect of character is illustrated by your display?

Image: Work – his hands. How you recall his hard skin and sores. Dirty nails. All seen when he was working in the shed, making a chair.

Of course, all this can be transferred to your own life and self. But notice how this emerged from notes and observation on an ordinary place: just a room in your house. In the end, your gratitude may be about security (the place) and love (your father – your love for him/his love for his carpentry)

The meaning of the writing, and its partly hidden purposes, will gradually be revealed.

At this point, you should record the fact that writing is often about the uneasy mix of pain and pleasure. The above exercise illustrates this well. Your stimulus was about a positive, feel-good factor such as being thankful. Yet in exploring this you uncovered loss and parting; you faced up to a lack in your life perhaps. The effort of revisiting a person who is no longer alive is painful, but naturally, it is related to the reasons why creativity exists.

Words can reveal what is hidden but felt. Your random reflections may in fact open up memories you had wanted to bury. But if they were born again in your words on the page, then clearly there is a deep reason why. Words can not only open up pain; they can ease it. They can even formulate new ways of relating to that emotional implosion which has lain unseen for a long time, pushed away in the process of everyday living. Your journal notes may even be beginning to shape towards writing for others, in spite of your purely personal need to explore selfhood and the nature of your complexity as a modern human being, existing in the accelerated present of the twentieth century, when the notion of permanence is dying.

Not so with your private writing, however. You are creating a permanent autobiographical account of how you are now, and what you aspire to be. If you have been honest, then this exercise will be totally revelatory to you. It began with a room and ended with a shifted perspective on your relationship with central elements of life such as place and the past.

Remember that your journal is a place for experimenting with thoughts and emotions, just as much as it is a resource for simply noting and listing items. You may find that re-reading material leads to further off-shoots which you didn't actually realise at the original time of writing. This is very much what we find in published notebooks by professional poets or novelists: the notebook is a series of false starts but often that is because the time was not 'right' for a specific idea to develop.

Checking on the skills so far

You have come a long way if you have come this far, and made your journaling an integral part of your life. Everything discussed about solitude relates to the basic psychological idea that the human being learns and grows most effectively by being involved with others – being in relationships. But this does not account for the lone artists who seem to need only themselves and 'their own company.' What skills have been offered so far in this book are a mix of communal and social, but the focus is on yourself alone.

This demands that you cultivate the virtues of silence, meditation and the encouragement of your own instinctive urges towards expression. One psychologist talks of our needing an 'empathically resonant self-object'. This usually means another person: one whom we can rely on for confirming our sense of self. But this thinker, Kohut, perhaps did not account for the nature of the past, or the imagination, or indeed personal phantasy as kinds of 'resonant self-objects.'

Of course, your journal is in the process of becoming exactly this – as if it were a friend, another 'self-object' like a mirror you can contemplate and decide what responses you feel about yourself as time passes. So what skills have you learned so far? When it comes to self-reflection, people of all ages, types and backgrounds record 'learning' in a variety of ways. For instance, it could involve a statement like one of these:

> *I've learned that when you want to cheer yourself up, you should cheer someone else up.*
> *I've learned that keeping a vegetable garden is worth a medicine cabinet full of pills.*
> *I've learned that everyone can use a prayer.*
> *I've learned that it pays to believe in miracles, and to tell the truth, I've seen several.*

In other words, whether the learning is do with skills or a body of knowledge,
there is no point in labelling one trivial and the other profound. You make your own wisdom. Therefore, before the expected skills are listed, write this piece of reflection:

Reflections

What kind of learning is important to you? Have you tended to absorb skills on courses or at school and college? What exactly do you think is 'learned' from friends and acquaintances? Is it your opinion that 'experience teaches fools' or do you think that all worthwhile things are learned through hard experience? This may all relate to your ability to make learning situations happen rather than drift into experience or even restrict your learning totally to structured experience. You might even want to write reflections on particular teachers you have had in your life.

Make your last journal entry for this chapter register some feelings about learning in your life and what you value in this, as well as what things you consider worthwhile. You could use these headings:

Things I learned on my own
Things I learned from friends
Worthwhile learning in formal situations

Your notes and reflections might have been related to purely factual items. If you did this, then note that skills may be transferable or marketable (like being able to drive or use a camera) but that also they may be instinctive, personal ones, such as inter-personal communication or creativity. You may have written down notes about your imagination and your ability to describe people vividly. This is quite acceptable. So many skills are hard to define. But here is a checklist of the expected skills you should have absorbed at this point:

- The ability to be objective about your attitudes
- Write descriptively about observed behaviour
- Preparation and receptivity for creative thinking
- How to instil a sense of order and ritual into self-reflection
- How to use language in order to access significance and meaning
- Using stimulus and memory-capture methods for 'workshop' techniques.

Don't worry if you can't confidently tick all these and smile with satisfaction. The important point is that you have probed into your deeper patternings of meaning and goals in life; you have also taken time to develop mental powers that you may never have known existed. The creative habits of thought and language-use now beginning to emerge are an even greater achievement.

People often say that learning by experience is always necessary, and this can lead to the depressing reflection that 'experience teaches fools' – a proverb often told to us in our youth. But a subject worth looking at is surely the nature of learning as adaptation. Your journal here might explore your changes – the radical changes in attitudes after significant failure or even shock. It should not be difficult to list those occasions in life which have taught you 'the hard way' and this may be compared with the learning you have done in a quite orthodox and painless way: the difference between learning formulae for maths and learning how to drive for instance. Mistakes in the former involve ink marks on paper, whereas mistakes in the latter might involve lives.

Case study

Paul was in need of a total re-think in his life. He was at a watershed. He had spent the first eight years of his career since graduating in Business Studies persevering with lower-level posts, with the belief that if he attended all the right seminars and listened to success-stories, then he would 'make it.' But he reached a stage of losing self-confidence and all sense of direction.

His response was to comb the library shelves looking for books about success by business gurus. He was looking for a pattern or a formula for success, and this always seemed to be measured in financial terms, or with criteria all about appearance, communication, sending out the right messages and so on.

Only by accident did he stumble on the idea of actually writing down what his frustrations were. He started this once in a café at lunch-time, after reading an account of writing therapy in a daily newspaper. All he did was write down things like words and phrases which seemed to irritate him or give him problems with self-esteem, and then add his own responses about his behaviour in this dilemma.

To his surprise, Paul found that, having written down clearly what was only messily evident in his mind, he began to express in speech, and then to see with more insight, exactly what course he should take. He learned that his lists and notes were actually about what were essentially 'spiritual' qualities (though not 'religious'). The result was that he applied some of these reflections in everyday social and communal situations, and a sense of honesty and faithfulness to his own ideals never caused any unrest or discontent.

Summary

This has been a crucially important chapter because you have been asked to delve more deeply and honestly into your personal resources as a creative person. The writing is still largely for your own benefit only, but we are moving towards giving you a profound insight into your 'hidden' skills and strengths as a person with almost infinite scope for imaginative expression. The chapter has also invited you to consider silence and solitude as elements in your learning profile

With this in mind, the focus on the 'workshop of one' idea has introduced these elements:

- Ordering your sessions with the journal
- Giving a sense of ritual to the activity – making writing special
- Pointing out that pain as well as pleasure is sometimes involved
- An insistence that there is a spiritual ingredient to all this.
- Development of the 'standing back' principle to show creative strengths

- Understanding a 'workshop' as a set of skills to be acquired, teaching yourself.

CHAPTER 8

Life-Writing

Everything you have done so far has been about dredging up words from deep down inside and making them work for you in the way you want them to work. This new life you are aiming at is one constructed of language, as it is the written and spoken word that lay foundations and also become architects of exciting new structures. What the next step involves is actually looking at the skills of writing about your life, so this is going to be about style and yet more verbal skills.

Introducing the new autobiographies

Writing about a life means writing about a self, and having a sense of self means that the writer exists in a world in which the individual counts for something. In the history of the West, many centuries passed before anyone really thought that an account of their inner life or childhood would be a subject for writing. The notion of autobiography was tied up with religious belief, as our passage through this life was only a preparation for a better life in Christian belief.

The changes came when particular writers moved from seeing life as a parable or lesson to life as a valuable individual testimony to how human experience and emotions may create happiness or its opposite. Rousseau, the French philosopher, began writing his "Confessions" in 1766, and thus produced the first piece of life-writing to really approach an understanding of our inner selves. He said, 'For what I have to say it is necessary to invent a language as original as my project.' In this he was anticipating the way we see life-writing now.

> *We can only deepen our reflective practices by envisaging our individual lives as part of the same adventure, of that always unfinished project for human fulfilment...*
> *however broken and uncertain it may now seem.*
> Peter Abbs

Rousseau was the first of several masters in life-writing whose achievements will prove useful in your own quest to find expression for your life-experience. He wrote about the motivations inside us, for good or evil, for pleasure or for pain.

In literature and philosophy, other major writer have contributed to how we write about ourselves. James Joyce and Virginia Woolf in the early year of this century, and Carl Jung in his writings about symbols and imagery also added to this exploration of how our memory and subconscious implodes into a mysterious chaos from which art and writing find a form. Freud's *The Interpretation of Dreams* has also been important. The result has been that when a writer begins to compose and assemble the fragments of life-data which will form the narrative, he or she is certain to be selective, and this is our starting-point for your journaling.

The new autobiographies work by:
- Accepting that anything is a fit subject
- Avoiding too much factual explanation
- Applying a controlling imagery
- Using language as something determining success or failure
- Accepting and using some film narrative techniques

The new autobiographies are the books of recent years which have broken with so many of the old rules about how you tell your own story. That is, why begin with birth and end with death? Why think of your life as an ordered structure, as if it were written like some Victorian novel? What writers do now is accept that experience is fragmentary, piecemeal, complex, and simply write as if they were a part of a total microcosm, not a directing presence.

Random responses

Now try an exercise that stems from these revolutionary working practices. This is to search for a significant object in your life and make it a large instrumental principle in the formation of your self. A simple way to do this is to imagine yourself as this object and then write without controlling the words.

Example:

Stage one: choose an object that could represent you. You might ask, 'If I were a fruit which one would I be? Or 'If I were a car, which model would I be?'

Stage two: Free-flow write yourself as that object

Stage three: study what you have said about your attitude to life and self by being that object.

A simple example would be if you chose a football as an object. You might be kicked, rolled through the mud, handled by a whole crowd of people, left in a dark shed when no longer needed – and so on. This free-flow writing is often poetic and provides an image for yourself.

Some masters explained

This is definitely the point in the course when some reading is going to be useful, before writing more. These are some summaries of famous autobiographers and what lies at the heart of their work that can be used by you.

Heraclitus   (died c.480 BC)

He concentrates on the puzzle and attraction of the 'I, thinking its thoughts now' – that is, the mystery of the self which creates and reflects. Our creating, responding self reflects the wonder and awe of the universe. He appreciated what we moderns think of as the 'self'. He said, most famously, 'You will not find the boundaries of psyche (the mind, the being) by travelling in any direction, so deep is the measure of it.'

What you can learn here:

1. Accept your uniqueness and your ultimate mystery. You write and express only what is accessible for that moment. The writing experience, then, is always continuing in a tunnel until the torchlight or oxygen gives out and you have to retrace your steps into the air.

2. Writing often has to settle for second-hand subjects and words. The truth of the actual life-data are often elusive, maybe even beyond any words.

Rousseau (1712-1778)

As the title implies, the attitude is one of revealing aspects of the self, as if opening up the truths of one individual account of what the nature of life really is. He tries to explain his own shortcomings and limitations, and ultimately wants to understand what elements form the foundations of a unique personality –as each of us is.

What you can learn here:
1. That the most tiny and seemingly insignificant detail of your experience is not to be taken for granted nor ignored. It is often the kernel of a plant waiting to grow.
2. Self-disclosure is often the best way to prove to oneself that particular experience or phases of life had a significance unrealised at the time.

Modernism (in particular the fiction of Virginia Woolf – 1882-1941)

In Modernism, a massive phase of literary history spanning the first two decades of this century, writers exploited the new interest in our subconscious following the translation of Freud's work into English at the turn of the century. The most intriguing thought being perhaps that, is we are so rich in our profoundly unknown inner selves, then surely this is just as interesting as our social and political behaviour?

Virginia Woolf's fiction often works from this basis, taking life as a flow of random experience: a 'stream of consciousness' which mixes important and trivial, logical and emotional data, and is often a fusion of what we put on life and what life lays on us. You have experienced day-dreaming, and so you have known these feelings.

What you can learn here:

1. Actively write about the moments in your day when concentration lapsed and your mind led you elsewhere!
2. Log and note your random thoughts and responses
3. Write about the way your mind keeps returning to constant preoccupations –and why?

How we learn from writers

Give some thought to the proposition that 'the readers we are determines the writers we become' and decide to what extent this applies to you. The idea of how we are influenced as writers is always interesting, as sometimes it is obvious, yet sometimes it is only evident on very close inspection of style. It may be that you are only influenced in the sense of a perspective on life, rather than anything in language and style. But you will be learning something valuable in your every act of creative reading.

This is exactly the point. Research has shown that reading is anything but passive. When you read, you are actively involved in the words and ideas; you maybe even indulge in a dramatic realisation of the word-painted scenes, and enlarge on the information given about character. If you have had that sensation of believing you have made a fictional character seem as real as 'people you know' then you are capable of writing such things yourself. Writers do several things for you as a writer:

1. They show how language can be generative of originality
2. They demonstrate how to transmute the ordinary into the magical
3. They illuminate the workings of imagination
4. They teach about using point of view and time-reference

There is much more, but the above is a useful starting-point for further thought. This is the perfect time to consider your learning in this context.

Reflections

Try to write a passage of writing – fiction or non-fiction – in the style and conventions of a particular genre or category. You might choose romance, thriller, spy, ghost story; or, you might choose non-fiction such as biography, local history, memoir, travel narrative, and so on. Write only a paragraph. Then write a paragraph next to this which is completely about yourself. *The only stipulation is that the passage has to be about names.*

The following is an example. Do not read these until you have tried your own.

1. genre passage:

   Mickey Delaney was just getting used to the office, but he was also trying to adapt to his new name. A private detective had to have a name with a certain sound to it. It had to sound tough. His real name, Alan Brown, just didn't seem right. It suggested a mild chap who arrives on the doorstep to sell your kitchen brushes. But Mickey Delaney – well, that guy had done time, packed a punch, took no nonsense from anyone.

2. Autobiography:

   They called me Peter, but not with any real thought. I mean, my parents were not religious, so there was no reference to the famous Christian. And they must have known I would be called 'Pete' by almost everyone. I've spent my life insisting on being called Peter and it's got me nowhere. Folk only think I'm a prig or a snob. It seems that only politicians or poets keep the full two syllables. A decent chap has to become a Pete and live up to the name.

Some feedback:

If you did this, notice that your writing demonstrated exactly how much you have learned from your reading. The above two passages prove that the writer has absorbed these abilities:

- Knowledge of the conventions of each passage
- Ability to choose the appropriate vocabulary
- The right tone for the narrative
- Use of sentence types and word order
- Use of stereotypes

You can learn a great deal from this. Look at what you have written in the autobiographical passage and ask yourself where those word-skills came from.

Patterning Life-Writing

Your journal and your writing habits are now quite sophisticated. They are also ordered and disciplined. It should be becoming second nature to you to write about yourself. But now you are going to apply some structures and techniques which move towards public writing – even doing material comparative to work in print. How do you give pattern and structure to autobiography? In your own responses and reflections so far, you have used some of these techniques. The basic skills are familiar:

- Using an image or symbol
- Working in a motif
- Using repetition
- Using contrast
- Selecting and rejecting data

Underlying all these skills is a well-established set of techniques. These are all summarised here, but are not intended as definitive, nor as all worth investigating. Simply try the ones that interest you.

1. *A Beliefs record*

List a number of beliefs you have had in the past but now do not. For instance, you may have changed from being optimistic in some things to being a realist. It may simply be something like:

That life always brings rewards

That hard work will always pay off

That people will always surprise you

And so on. Write about twenty of these, and then the next step is obviously to explore your reasons for discarding these beliefs.

2. *Plans and reality*

This can be extended into a list of statements about someone, covering the main stages in their life, in this way:

My father

Born into a poor family

Wanted to become a musician

Worked hard at music in school

In his teens, left school early – family needed money

He had little time for piano

Married at 20

Worked as a retail manager

This leaves out so much. It leaves out the emotional fabric of the man's life. It must also be typical of so many lives, illustrating as it does the disappointment, frustrations and fateful circumstances around us all the time. But apply the principle to your own life, of course.

3. *Portraits*

Write a pen-sketch of someone close to you. Practise the skills of recording the individual features, and use their everyday habits as a basis, in this way:

John: always has toast and jam for breakfast/ spills coffee on the table/ comments on the Third World/ talks about all the garden jobs to be done/ tends to scratch his nose when nervous etc.

Notice how this is an excellent starting-point for any future life-writing, and for your own autobiographical work, as it concentrates on the visual and tactile details. It has a basis in human senses and movement as well as appearance.

Notes

In your journal, put together all the most attractive elements of the above exercises. A potentially revelatory way to do this is to write an imagined dialogue with another person. The person may be real or imagined, relative or friend. It may even be 'another self' which is past of you – a second version of you that did something else in life. For instance:

Me: Oh, here we go again. A visit from my father. He's moaning all the time.

#2 What makes him moan? Do you ever turn his attention away?

Me: It's too late now. He's seventy years old

#2 So you give up – that's no answer.

Just write, following your instincts, then reflect on the finished piece and what it tells you.

Using a classic: Plato's cave

Much of this chapter has been about your perceptions of yourself and others, largely from a specific stance, often biased and so well established that it has never been questioned. The same judgements will be applied to you by others. The fact is that we can never 'see' the total reality around us, and writers simply celebrate and express wonder at the images they do confidently see.

It is helpful here to introduce one of the oldest ideas on how we see life, coming from the classical Greek philosopher, Plato (427-347 BC). In his work, *The Republic*, he explains the limitations of how and what we see as the metaphor of people being trapped in a dark cave, from which they see, with light flickering on the wall, the outlines of the figures passing by outside the cave. The results are, naturally, that our perception of the world is

1. Distorted
2. Second-hand
3. Imagined and constructed by our minds

4. Subject to revision with every figure we see

If we apply this to art and writing, the result is that there are ways of seeing, and a writer simply concentrates on one – however unsound and suspect the veracity of the vision may be. We accept distortions as part of the game.

This can be used in all kinds of ways. You can take the parable of passing figures as a way of interpreting your life and the people you have met in the past, and who have walked on into the darkness. It can even be developed as an image of the connotations of the word 'see'. This little word is used in dozens of different ways, and each is a basis for writing in that it informs the writer about these necessary limitations, as in 'I see what you mean' or I didn't see the danger coming' or ' Let's see if he'll change'

Case study

Jill had returned to college locally, as a mature student. She wanted to find out what she was good at, so she did a general 'Access' course which would give her an introduction to a range of subjects in social science. Yet the more she listened to and read interpretations of life in communities, accounts of urban crime and drug problems in cities, the more she began to revise and revisit her own past life – something she had never done before with any system.

It proved to be her saving, as she had found that the very long and dull textbooks, packed with academic jargon, appeared to have very little to do with the life she had known. Her family had seemed so normal, with no real problems at all; she had never been involved in petty crime, or had difficulties with morality. Her friendships had all been sound and comforting – most of them lasting into adulthood. She began to wonder if there was something wrong with her for not having anything wrong...

What opened her mind to what social studies really offered was reading about oral history. She read a project in which housewives during the second world war spoke about their lives for an oral history project called Mass Observation. Jill realised that the 'data' a student uses could indeed be something with an ordinary human basis, and that seemingly uneventful lives were run through with tragedy as well as with joy.

Jill purposely started to use her own family history, and kept a log of her findings in the archives. She found herself writing about poverty in the thirties in Leeds where her family originated, and she even compared her findings with similar research in print.

This opened up a world of expression she had never thought about before. It was only a small move to go from that writing to producing reflections on her own existing relatives, so interviewing her grandmother opened up new perspectives on Jill herself – things she wanted to express in the written word. Social studies then seemed to be about people rather than statistics, after all.

Summary

This chapter has been about the ways in which different versions of life-writing may have a beneficial effect on your own reflections. There has been a revolution in the perceptions of autobiography this century in psychology and literature, and this has had a knock-on effect on creative writing and art. Some of these techniques are easily absorbed into your daily journaling practice and the exercises here are all related to the main theme of this book – seeing yourself afresh and rebuilding a sense of self and the confidence that goes with it.

The topics covered have been:
- Looking at what you read and why
- The development of fluency in writing style
- Confidence with writing about people
- Using the skills of life-writing

- Considering some classical statements about life-writing
- Noting and acting on the idea of self and individuality

CHAPTER 9

Bridging your career and your creativity

This is a crucially important stage of the working towards your new life. You may not realise it, but your writing habits have now gone beyond the level of an opening towards expressing yourself, and into possibilities of public writing. That is, if you have accepted the journaling and all its potential, you will most certainly find yourself in possession of an impressive amount of written material. You might want to bring this creative habit rather more directly into your life.

In fact, it will be hard to resist doing this by now, so this chapter is about your creative self in the broader sense.

Being creative in all departments

If you kept up with the reflections and notes, and faithfully tried the experiments in autobiography in these, you will have realised that there is a constant assumption that we all have a creative self, and that this self can be accessed and so enrich your 'surface' life in work, family, career and relationships. Now, regardless of how you define 'career', the time has come to take a closer look at this creativity.

An interesting way to do this is to sketch a map – a particular kind of map that places you in relation to all the major influences on your life, but the context is in your creative nature itself. Let's call this the Map of Imagination. Follow this process:

Map of Imagination

Think about yourself as a child and place your name in the centre of a page of A4 paper. Then, in places around this, write all the areas in which you were asked to be creative, or in fact were spontaneously creative, following your own desires in play and so on.

You might have something like this, *with the important distinction of writing in capitals the sources of your imaginings made by you alone.*

Stories of ghosts and fairies   second-hand clothes

YOUR OWN BEDTIME STORIES

Drawing book…. . …… **Jenny**----------------doll's house

OLD HOUSE

Stories read at school   art project

Fig. 3   Map of Imagination

The idea behind this is that you are forced to recapture the sources of imagination that you actually made for your own uses. In the example above, just think what the imaginative uses to which the OLD HOUSE was put. Did Jenny explore this, seeing in the ruins ghosts of past generations? Did she imagine she heard a child crying in a dark corner? When you have written your map, give some real thought to the things in capitals, then extend your memories and write further notes.

Notes

With your map of imagination in mind, now give some thought to what happened to you at times which involved your creative acts – in art lessons, at home telling stories and so on. List any occasions you can think of, and next to each one, note the responses at the time from friends, parents, teachers or anyone else who knew about what you were doing. Some of these memories might be negative:

friends may have teased you for being 'dreamy' and 'in a world of your own', yet on the positive side, you may have been complimented for being a good storyteller.

List at least three such occasions and add reflective notes. It may involve very unpleasant memories for some, such as actually being punished for being creative – even punished for *poor* writing or drawing. Include all the creative arts, not only creative writing here.

> *Writing is a word conveying power as well as peace. We write truths which may not be spoken, and when we write things down, we add a sense of permanence. Writing makes thoughts count for more.*

Acquiring learning habits

You might be wondering what kinds of learning have been progressing as you have followed the exercises so far. The fact is that learning itself will happen continuously in everything you do, but that writing, being a special skill, involves particular abilities in a given situation.

For instance, supposing you write about one of the experiences from childhood mentioned above in the map of imagination. That effort to revisit a certain personal past involves a massive amount of learning. To recreate that experience on paper requires these skills:

- Evocation of the scene for others
- Empathy with the 'you' that was then – a different self
- Finding adequate words to express the reality
- Applying a structure and development of the scene/feeling etc.
- Recalling the voice, words, tastes, sounds etc. of the scene

Notice how your learning habits in writing and creativity rely almost totally on these functions of recall and recreation. The link between memory and imagination is well established, but each individual has to develop the methods of working with these things for him or herself. Examples of how learning habits become tried and tested in writing are easy to find, as so many writers talk about their research and preparation techniques in interviews. It is even possible to read journals by some writers, actually in print, sometimes reproduced in facsimile.

You can learn from this, and it is helpful here to look at ways in which writers access this learning when required. In everyday language, this is called perhaps 'material.' Writers will talk about looking for their material, but this is just the beginning of that transmutation which goes on in their minds. Jack Higgins, for instance, once said that his wife didn't understand that, if he was staring out of the window, apparently dreaming, he was still 'working' on his current novel.

This is an example of the processes which are involved in learning habits for creativity:

Stage 1   A period of excitement as a mental 'goal' is stated – to oneself perhaps.

Stage 2   A latent period in which formations in the artistic medium are made

Stage 3   A rush of activity to record the imaginative excitement of creating something original.

Stage 4   A colder, more objective view of work done, and plans for more meaningful structuring are made.

For writers, the second stage is the crucial one, as at this point, you may be aware of all kinds of disparate thoughts and data mixing and coming together. Writers often speak about ideas gradually becoming 'right' but when this is exactly remains vague. The proper time to sit down and write the first page simply happens. The latent stage often involves dreams, as the mind is coping with intractable ideas as the subject matures; dreams may clarify an issue, such as resolving some plotting or character relationship for a novelist.

For your purposes, this breaks down to three key learning habits for writing:

- Allowing a chosen subject time to mature
- Recording the progress in your journaling habits
- Letting the creativity come before the need to order

The last point is all about the revision and re-writing stage, when the chaos of imaginative flow has been logged in some way, and then a shaping must happen. Any of your journal entries could have the potential for this development.

Opening up new routes

Creativity is haphazard. It is part of that chaotic unknown element in us, completely vague and defying definition. It is significant in being the road to innovation, but it can also function as a clarifying principle, as it may be an inner mess searching for a healthy order. Suffering works in this way of course, and the link between the emotional life and the creative state of being is very strong.

Think of your imaginative resources as being like a transport system. The motorways of your thought and feeling are very well used and sometimes are too efficient.

They take care of all the necessary survival thinking for home and job. Then the A roads: they have a prominent use as well, feeding those aspects of your life and self which are used fairly often., perhaps as routine or occasional roles and duties.

But the B roads: what about them? These are the routes into that power of imagination in you. The B roads lead to little-known or utterly unknown regions of you. They may go to obscure memory, beloved ritual, people from the past who still come into mind and so on. How do you ensure that these B-roads are not disused, left off the map, as it were?

The answer, of course, is regular use? Use roads and they remain in use. So in your writing, keep these roads well-used and in repair. This is done by inviting randomness and chance in even the smallest things.

Random responses

A constructive way to keep this habit going is to have a keyword in your journal every day. This keyword is the code for opening up your writing after that particular day's events and thoughts. For instance:

Keyword: Happiness

Start with questions about time/place/people etc. that make or gave made you happy.

Move on to other related words, just by mental association. List ten words that relate to happiness *for you*.

Finally, choose one of these related words and write about it as if explaining it to an alien with no concept of the word or thing. This will force you to revisit the concept as if it were new. Even a simple thing such as a candle-lit dinner for two will bring some surprising results, as it forces you to express your pleasure in the experience.

Games for success

As was noted in the first chapter, the centre of creativity is play. In your writing, make time for actively playing with the possibilities of words. We all need to look at the resonances and connotations of words if we are to use them creatively. For example, a word such as HARM:

- resonances: these are the echoes of meaning simply from the sound and use of the word. It is an ancient word, Germanic in origin, very simple and powerful in use. What does it suggest?

- Connotations: this refers to the range of effects the use of the word causes. Notice how you can use the word to show extremes, as in 'harmful substance' or to do' grievous bodily harm' to someone. Or, in opposite sense, someone can have fun and 'mean no harm'.

You can also imagine words as animals or imaginary beings. What animal would a LIAR be? Or a GATEKEEPER?

The most powerful way to energise your words is to play with the way you use them and the order in which you use them. Writers often take this to an extreme by inventing words, combining existing ones, as in Lewis Carroll's poems: we feel we know what a 'slithy tove' is in the opening lines of 'Jabberwocky':

> *'Twas brillig and the slithy toves*
> *did gyre and gimble in the wabe;*

and, in context, it is easy to guess what the other invented words are meant to suggest.

Equally, writers can add meaning to already existing, mundane words just by changing them slightly: Roger McGough has a poem called 'The Heath Forecast' in which he talks about the geography of the body.

In other words, successful writing depends on how you transform the dying language into new, vibrant usage and meanings. In your journal, make an attempt to do this by writing a paragraph about a word you think is over-used and make it interesting. A word such as 'pressure' for instance, could be imagined as an animal.

The point is that good prose is capable of anything you want it to express, if the words are alive; and they will be alive if you take time over them.

> *When I examine my mind and try to discern clearly in the matter, I cannot satisfy myself that there are any such things as poetical ideas. No truth, it seems to me, is too precious, no observation too profound, and no sentiment too exalted to be expressed in prose.*
> A.E. Housman

Using the past in the present

As has been said so many times in previous chapters, your past is your greatest reserve. It is a territory known only to you, and understood only in your way. Therefore, those B roads into sites of creativity need to be enlightened, mapped out in all their detail. By making a special profile of yourself and your sources in your past, you can deepen your writing about yourself and about the changes you need in your life.

Your Self-Source

This is a suitable name for your own profile extending into your origins, as it is about what you have inherited in various categories. You work on the simple device of sentence-completion. Begin with these:

Father – I am most like/unlike my father in……..

Mother- I am most like/unlike my mother in….

Now move on to these:

Past people- I most miss……… because……

I miss ……… very little because…

This basic formula can be applied to other things from your past such as places and influences. You should discover, in the process of doing this, that aspects of the past provide some of those B-road sites. Your self-source may be mainly located there.

However, what if you dismissed most of the more distant past, such as your childhood, as having little importance for your self-source now? Maybe the most defining aspects of yourself now are in fact quite recent? You may have placed recent friendships as being more important for you than past relationships with family members. There is nothing unusual in this.

But this section is about *using* the past. How do writers use the past? There seem to be three basic strategies here:

1. As material – something only they know about.
2. As a way of enlightening the present.
3. As a shared image of happiness, escape or pain.

In other words, in your journaling, use the past when it figures in some present solutions. Mostly, these are about motivations. If you pose the question: what motivates me most? The answers are often in the past. You may feel that the lessons of an earlier generation have been learned. You may wish to do the opposite of what parents did. These comparisons and contrasts, as means of enlightening the way your life is going now, provide excellent journal material.

Case study

Jane was a member of a creative writing class, and she had started the course because she wanted to write her autobiography. For several weeks, the group read several standard, classic autobiographies, and there seemed to be no method or formula. The writer simply followed the pattern of life, growth and change. In fact, she wasn't really sure that she wanted to write for anyone else. The other students seemed to be preoccupied with seeing their work in print.

Jane was at the stage at which she knew that writing about her life and self was all she wanted; the other students were mostly novelists and poets. What she was learning was predominantly about writing for an audience. But it was that first step in confidence and a sense of self in the words that she wanted to see and achieve.

It was during a session on writing character that she saw what was required. Everyone talked about 'researching characters' and basing fictional people on real people. During a discussion on this, she realised that one reason why she had the urge to write was to understand – mostly to understand her parents and her childhood. She had been brought up in a family atmosphere in which important emotional subjects were not openly discussed.

She simply recreated a scene from reality in a class exercise: one in which, during a family bereavement, an uncle had spoken openly about his feelings for the first time. The other students thought it was brilliant fiction. It had that feel of authenticity, because she had revisited the moment of that revelatory talk in a family setting.

From that point, Jane knew that she could write well about her own people and about how she had grown into adulthood in spite of that communication failing. Writing about the absence of honest expression opened up the doors to her creativity.

Summary

> *In this chapter the emphasis has been on experimentation. You are at the stage at which you need to review your use of words: to combat the over-familiarity of them. Journaling involves not only recording events and responses, but trying to reflect the authentic experience. The necessary creative abilities are tractable and may be learned, perhaps with the difficulty of learning a musical instrument. But, as with the latter, practice and constant use is the key to success.*

The chapter has covered:

- Deepening your enquiries into your personal history
- Learning strategies for accessing your self-source
- Practising the skills with manipulating words needed for authentic writing
- Opening up the play element in writing.

CHAPTER 10

Writing Poems for Yourself

Much of what has been discussed and suggested to you so far has been profoundly concerned with accessing your unconscious knowledge and your life data. It must come as no surprise to learn that poetry, of all the verbal arts, is the one most suited to matching those imaginative impulses we have been calling on in the exercises. Poetry is something running parallel to the spontaneous response to life: its beauties as well as its brutality and callousness.

This chapter aims to show how writing poetry, even in its most simple forms, as part of your journaling, will increase the power of your expression and the depth of your self-reflections.

Poems and being spontaneous

Poetry is a much misunderstood art. Many writers seem to consider it the most amateur of the verbal arts, perhaps because so many people can write adequate rhymes and plain messages in rhythm. But as a real craft, poetry is very difficult to learn in terms of its technical aspects. Here, you will learn a little of this, but the focal interest for you now is to use poems as part of your overall access to your own language. Writing poems is so useful for this because it is writing that reduces statements to a minimum; it condenses and refines words down to reflecting the essence of experience.

People writing poetry for the first time are often held back by ideas of intellectual depth. Maybe this is because there is an element in the poetry world of the snobbish division of *poetry and verse.* The emergence of performance poetry has complicated this even further, by showing that poetry can be as entertaining as pop music or stand-up comedy. Basically, just believe in the foundation of poetry as being in a sort of 'under-voice'. This is the intonation of your own which directs you to take up a certain attitude in your composition.

This under-voice is the expression of your spontaneity. A useful way to become aware of this is to write freely, simply in prose, on a subject you feel strongly about, and add a tone of irony or sarcasm. That creates a very obvious kind of attitude. But there is a simple way to give your poem a spontaneous feel, and yet use a simple form. This is to use *syllabics.* This means to write statements with particular line-lengths, made up of syllable-counts, like this: *Like rain on chalk I wash you from my day.*

You always did take all your love away.
Now I'm done. Can't take any more.
You cut my soul and I feel sore.

The syllable counts here is 10/10/8/8, but you can make any patterns of line-length you like such as 4/4/6/6/8/8/ or 3/3/5/5/2/2/. The permutations are maybe endless, but what this does is force an attitude and helps you to sense this under-voice which dictates a poem to you p structures it according to your attitude to the subject. This form of writing is technically 'formal' but follows our natural intonations of expression.

Another guideline for free poetry is to simply write according to a series of moods, writing a short piece each time you sit down to journal. Over say ten days, a series of short reflections on a subject which is bothering you or interesting you, will shape up into something substantial.

Free and formal

A basic concept to consider first is whether to write in any accepted form of poem, or to write freely. A free verse poem is one that allows the inner rhythms of your thinking and feeling to come through directly, the words following the emotional tenor of your genuine responses. Formal poetry is about words put into particular frames of rhyme, rhythm and visual pattern. For instance, you might see someone begging in the town centre. Your first response might be put in free verse like this:

1. Basic feelings as in your head at the time:

    ' He holds out the bowl like Oliver Twist. But I bet he's never seen a workhouse. Probably has a Jaguar parked around the corner.'

2. Written as free verse:

    ' Never seen a workhouse, and a Jag

    just a street away. But he begs like Oliver Twist.

    Asking for more, when he's got enough.'

3. You could, alternatively, work in rhymes and give it a form:

    'He's never seen a workhouse, and a Jag

    a street away, but he holds a tote- bag,

    scratches at a louse and keeps pride at bay.'

Here, notice how each line has ten stressed syllables, and look at where words are rhymed – both at the end of lines and in the middle of lines. The overall effect is one of attractive sound qualities for the reader or listener.

The point to make here is that what really counts is the spontaneous, direct response to your experience. Whether or not you choose to work on the immediate language and create the formal elements of poetry is your choice. We will look at some simple examples.

Note here, however, that in modern poetry, there are no demands that you should know the traditional forms such as sonnets or villanelles. What does count for a great deal is the ability to make your writing have the authentic feel – words based on genuine feelings.

> *Poetry is properly speaking a transcendental quality – a sudden transformation which words assume under a particular influence – and we can no more define this quality than we can define a state of grace...*   Glyn Jones

Notes

To grasp what is meant by the immediacy of poetic writing – its spontaneous expression – try this writing exercise in your notebook.

Stage one

From a quiet place such as a library or a restaurant, watch a human scene: any place where a crowd of people will gather. A market is always full of potential for this. But equally, a bus-queue or a crowd at a sporting event would be ideal.

Stage two

Write every word and phrase that comes into your mind simply as a description of what behaviour and detail you see. This could include clothes, faces, what they carry, the movements they make and so on.

Stage three

Decide on making three areas of your subject such as 1. The atmosphere/weather   2. The queue or crowd   3. A specific person

Then write in prose sentences on each one of these, using your notes.

Stage four

Finally, simply write half of each sentence as a line of poetry, so you might have something like this:

Notes: wearing an old cardigan. Looks like a refugee. Carrying tatty string bag. Wears a scruffy trilby hat. Genteel – maybe European. Foreign-looking.

Free verse:

He wears a trilby. Stands waiting like a refugee.
The string bag clutched in the thin hand.
So genteel, somehow foreign. Doesn't belong there.

Notice how the detail from observation is enough. You need to add very little to your original, spontaneous responses. Immediacy involves helping your reader to that exciting sense of sharing your experience as he or she reads. The white space between lines, the rhythms and the changes of intonation all help to create this sense of the reader's involvement.

The Poet's Notebook

If you find that you want to make writing poetry a prominent ingredient in your journaling, then start keeping a small notebook – one that would fit easily in a pocket or small bag. Most writers use this anyway, as observation is crucial to the art. A notebook is essential for these reasons:

- Logging the passing response
- Sharpening your powers of observation
- Drafting out images
- Assembling themes and subject in parts
- Storing the potentially creative journaling topics

Of course, keeping a notebook is also part of the basic equipment of a writer. It often contains merely scraps and drafts of things that never quite worked out, but it reflects a habit of thought.

Above all, never think that poetry is only for highbrow art, and that it is concerned with the intellect rather than the emotions. The assumption of this book is that made in many non-European concepts of poetry – that is, poetry is expression open to anyone and is about actual reality. It is about life and its duties and beauties: not necessarily about inner contemplation, though it may also be that.

Your attitude must be that of sharing the experience of all humanity. The celebration of joy depends on noticing the power and delight in what is ordinary and often ignored. The notebook is the place for making sure that your honest words are recorded, even if you play with them later. There is a distinction in art between 'truth and design' that is fundamental to the notebook idea:

Truth:

The essential, factual data as observed.

Design:

Your artifice – the way you develop that basic material into a form or into literary expression. Notice, for instance, what a simple adjective can do when added to a basic fact: ' The house was on the lonely heath'. Insert the word 'deserted' before 'house' and you add something giving more significant detail.

It may be that your poems are no more than meditations, expressed at random and according to mood, but this is fine. Rules are the enemies of creativity and your imagination needs to push any rules aside if it is to work without the burdens of the schoolroom or 'the system'.

Your journal has all the main aspects of a poet's notebook, the only difference being that you are probably not thinking primarily on the final draft being published. This is a good point at which to consider how you feel about writing for others as well as yourself. After all, your journal is your listener and confidant. It only takes one more step to another reader, and you have extended things considerably.

Another interesting example of how a notebook raises the levels of creativity is in the printed case studies of writers' notebooks actually available for us to read, and to see the writing process in action. What tends to happen in writing poetry is that the accidental, the ideas arriving by chance and sheer serendipity, are often more successful than the planned and structured writing. A good example is the story about the American poet, Robert Frost. He was working hard on a poem about New Hampshire, sitting at his desk and striving for what he wanted; but it was failing. He walked out on the porch and the words of one of his most famous poems formed in his head and almost 'wrote itself' – a poem called *Stopping by Woods*.

> Saw the ice on the shed roof today (Dec.12.) like bony fingers. Kids were making a snowman. Nose made from a pencil. Laughter was like a football rattle. Thought about the current story – based on my dad but with some elements of my old schoolteacher, Mr. Cheshire. Innocent, returns from the war to find his home village totally changed. Poem or story? Could be done as either.
>
> n.b.
>
> FIND OUT ABOUT THE PETERLOO MASSACRE. Check library. Find details about who was there, and what happened after. 1819 – just after war with Napoleon. Would make a tremendous narrative poem.
>
> Note: Saw the old lady with the plastic bags again. Where does she sleep at nights? This weather will kill her. How to write about her? As a monologue?

Fig. 4   Page of a poet's notebook

Generating images

A successful way to develop your subjects for poetry, directly from your own life and your past, is to study a checklist of potential sources of imagery, as all poetry depends on the images by which the poetic statements work. For instance, the basic idea of a poetic statement is to say something in a non-literal way:

Literal: *The sun rising over the sea made the sky pale orange.*

Figurative (using an image): *The sun's rays were wheel-spokes turning orange with their magical journey into day.*

In other words, you need some idea on how to access the infinite stock of imagery contained in your brain. This is such a massive store because you have been recording and storing impressions since you first looked at and responded to the sensual beauty of the world. Here are some devices you could use to generate poetic imagery:

List comparisons of objects or people

Write imagined monologues

- Describe things as if they were alien
- Write as if an object were speaking
- Treat aspects of life as symbols – e.g. what animal would 'Fear' be?

- Use photographs and paintings to start your own pen-sketches
- Use registers of language – e.g. a tannoy, a letter to a teacher, an ansaphone, as ways of writing.

More could be added. The technique here is to adopt a voice for the poem different from your own. The last item on the list makes a useful example. Suppose you were to write about your love for someone. Instead of the usual sonnet, why not write as if the poem were the message on the ansaphone? For instance:

' Look, I know you're there.
You're washing your hair
As they say, in a polite way
Of saying get lost, I've had enough.
Well call me back, I'm feeling rough.
Without you, there's just night and no day.'

You can try these practice exercises in any of countless registers of everyday language use. Remember that a register is simply a way of talking or writing in a certain context. Think of how many different registers you use in a typical day:

1. Writing a note for the milk person.
2. Talking on the phone to a friend.
3. Writing an e-mail

4. Talking to a toddler in the street
5. Making comforting noises when listening to someone who is ill.
6. And so on, in a multitude of ways every day. The important thing here is to note your honest responses to experience. You will be amazed how many of these are expressed in imagery or in powerful ways.

Random responses

In your journal, try some poetry on the theme of an unwritten letter. Imagine that you are writing to someone and saying something that you want to say, or wanted to say in the past but the opportunity has gone. It can be serious or playful. Write your thoughts as prose first, then into free verse, using the method above, making each prose sentence into two lines of verse, like this:

Prose sentence: I wanted to say how much I missed our talks over hot coffee in that out café by the sea. It was always cold in there. Cold as hell, but you always warmed up the day for me.

Free verse lines:

How much I miss our talks. I want to say
How much I miss the hot coffee in the cold room,
And you warming me, with the chill sea outside.'

The actual attempt to write in the register of a letter imposes a certain attitude, and also allows for the scope of using an existing convention in writing in a new way. A classic example is what is known as 'staircase wit' – the things you wanted to say when you were talking, or at an interview, but only thought of the right words when leaving the office and went away down stairs. This even gives you a formal arrangement such as:

I wanted to say…… but I was silent
I should have said….. but I was tongue-tied

Notice how even a simple set on contrasts like this creates a lot of stylistic interest and possibilities for wit and double-meaning.

But the important point about random responses is that they most often do not work out: when they do it is wonderful, but never despair. Patience has its rewards, and they often come in writing with a meteor, not a slow-burning fire.

Surprise and shock: inner stories

Poetry is ideal for those areas of your life which, although personal and special to you, have a universal importance. In your writing, there will be moments at which you feel the need to express aspects of the truly eternal verities of life's fundamental nature. After all, birth, belief, parting, death and transcendent vision are the stuff of all poetry since it was first related to song. The elemental stories are poetic, as in the great classical epics and even in the folksongs which still have a resonance for modern men and women.

Obviously, all writing also deals in basic methods of interest also: surprise and shock are part of the standard repertoire in popular fiction and in more serious literature. A strong presence in your own writing of this elemental subject will make your journaling face up to some of the fundamentals of your beliefs. Most of these stories tend to be parables, fantasies and allegories: that is, they tell simple stories but have a profoundly rich meaning when interpreted.

An example would be like this:

1. List all the experiences in your life which you feel reflect your hardest, most demanding challenges. You might have a range of things from learning to swim despite being teased to coping with bereavement.
2. Choose one of these experiences and break down all the elements involved. For instance, losing a best friend or relative might give rise to these experiences:

Isolation

Lack of purpose in life

Questioning of God or benign providence
A sense of depression and futility
A revision of your life's decisions and achievements

3. Write about the aspect you have chosen in such a way that you are distanced from the events and feelings. In other words, write in the third person- he/she. You might have this:

' Tom felt desolate as he looked up at the heavens and felt the immensity of the cosmos. He had lost a dear friend and he would never see him again. He felt so small, so insignificant. Nothing seemed worthwhile if all effort and work came to this – just a sudden ending of everything and oblivion.'

4. Finally, recall what it was that reclaimed you to life, as it were: what brought you back to a sense of affirmation , back into the participation in life you now hopefully have regained? It may have been simply watching a child play. So place side by side the heart of both experiences – the desolate and the affirmative. This is a parable in miniature; a story of a return to life after despair.

As a poem, these inner stories make powerful writing. They contain in a short form some of the mightiest struggles we have to face in life. Something like the story of George and the Dragon is the type of interest you should create. But of course the story is actually about you. It's just that you distance the perspective and point of view to make it universal.

This will be a step towards public writing, but it is still essentially personal journaling in order to understand the emotional and imaginative blocks in life, and to move on positively. After all, affirmation is perhaps more difficult for us to do than desperation. Comedy seems to be tougher than misery on writing courses, and possibly it is quite hard work to search out the affirmative feelings, as in everyday small talk we so often relate to each other in terms of grumbling and complaining. This is where poetry has a very important contribution to make in life: what the poet Philip Larkin called 'An enormous yes' when he tried to express how wonderful the music of the jazz saxophonist Sydney Bechet made him feel.

Your own 'enormous yes' is an affirmation that life is valuable when understood properly as joy, as laughter in the face of mystery and complexity.

Practising the art of haiku

One of the most affirmative and pleasurable aspects of writing poetry is the way the act of concentrating thoughts and feelings relates to meditation and vision. Think about times in which you have watched something small and insignificant which has led to your seeing something profound. As William Blake said, 'to see eternity in a grain of sand' is an experience common to poets if they cultivate a certain way of seeing reality.

Oriental art and writing often has such qualities, and one of the most helpful for you now is the art of *haiku*. In Japan, the three-line poem, the haiku, is a meditation on beauty or nature. It simply describes a mood, a scene or a passing feeling. The haiku tradition involved a journey something like a retreat in religion. The poet went ot the hills on a prescribed route, and kept a haiku notebook of things observed on the journey. So it entailed a certain sense of using the journey as a parable for life itself, and was only fitting that the observations made were about the richness and fascination of life. The haiku has three lines with a syllable count of 5 –7-5 as in this example:

Bending in the field,
Workers pull from the dead earth
Life in winter's chill

Notice how this only really describes. It doesn't have to rhyme either. The idea is to discipline your expression by putting a boundary on your thinking, using the limitations to refine your use of words to exactly what you see and say, and no more.

The process is simply to write in prose first, producing a short paragraph of description, and then extract the three lines, editing down to the syllable-count. Suitable subjects for a haiku might be:

- Watching a child play
- The simplicity of cooking
- A landscape in a particular season
- Animal behaviour
- Attractive and sensual objects
- A specific time of day in town or county

Remember that a haiku reflects a way of seeing the natural world in an innocent way: simply being aware of *being rather than having*. Arguably, the West has become too concerned with having, owning, being master of something. In contrast, the meditation of haiku and other short poems involves observation and reflection on learning from simplicity. The act of looking is sensuous in itself, and it needs nothing cerebral, nothing analytical. A typical example would be this:

> *Summer wears red dresses:*
> *Shows the starry bracelets well.*
> *Who thinks of the dead?*

Here, the last line draws a simple question. But the poem begins with an observation. Often, when given a first line that simply describes something, a poem opens out. To add to your journaling routine, you could even write just one opening descriptive line each time to sit down. A typical example might be:

Under green cover

Notice how this invites you to add a following line with an *action*, building on a mere image. The art of haiku is a discipline in itself, making you condense your thoughts and focus on what is essential in the life around you, and helping you to think in a *writerly* way.

Reflections

For the last exercise in poetry, try to write a haiku based on the subject of a room. Take the room in which you sit down to write your journal. Write a paragraph on this, using three or four objects in the room which you feel are specially attractive or significant for you. This would be an example:

The room has a large, wide window with a dangling glass sun-catcher. On the sill there is a tall pink vase, bending and spiralling like a child's slide. The autumn light is trapped in the leaves of a coleus on a small table.

This could be worked into three lines like this:

The glass sun-catcher
Dances in the autumn light:
The coleus blushes.

Note that the art of this lies in the compression of the original notes into succinct lines which encapsulate your meditation. But the art of haiku may be much simpler. Basically, if you tire of the 5-7-5 format, just forget it and write three lines that have an attractive cadence and rhythm. That will be enough to satisfy the need for poetic form.

Case study

Colin was well into his writing now, and he was at the stage at which he was thinking about trying to have work published. He read some small magazines, as writing stories and poetry was his main interest. But his journaling was mainly about looking at himself, not communicating to others. He felt that, before he actively tried public writing, he should attempt something which made him explore the inner identity much more acutely.

He had this sense that the self was something that kept escaping, like the gestures and signs made along the way in life- waving and clapping and hitching a lift – just movements, with no real sense of self at all. His reflective writing had not taken him to any convincing recognition of what his 'self' was at all.

Colin came to realise that it was in poetry that this was tackled most transparently. There were lots of poems in anthologies and collections which tried to explore the deeper sense of being – almost a religious sense. He tried oriental forms, and poems such as the haiku provided him with the challenge of saying only the absolute minimum, sloughing off any unwanted and extra thoughts which were not needed in the thinking behind the writing. He absorbed a great deal of general writing technique without realising it.

The result was a testing discipline which had him playing the mental game of syllable-counting, and shuffling around the syntax of his normal writing. It was eventually well worth the effort. Haiku forced him to slim down his tendency to think, talk and write at inordinate length. The effort to observe and to note only essential features even had a beneficial effect on his concentration and listening. In fact, he learned that the effort to start each day's journal writing with a haiku made him focus more attentively and successfully on the theme that had preoccupied him in the day. It became his 'warming-up' technique for writing.

When he did decide to write for publication, he had a stock of short poems to start with, and to develop when needed.

Even a short piece of formal writing like a haiku satisfied the question about 'writing for what reason' that had troubled him. Only by submitting to the discipline did he win some valuable knowledge.

Summary

In this chapter the main point of interest has been to look at how writing poetry can enhance your journaling and your general notebook-keeping. We began by asking what the value of spontaneous writing was, and how the very nature of imaginative writing is to change and to constructively transmute the actual stuff of existence.

Poetry is akin to meditation, and is an art that is open to use in religious and philosophical contexts. You were asked to try your skills at writing from notes and drafts with these points in mind:

- Writing poetry is a skill to enrich your expressive powers
- The art of poetry is to reduce, to crystallise thought and feeling
- The distinction between form and free verse is important

- The heart of poetic vocabulary, imagery, can be cultivated.
- Keeping a notebook is an essential habit.
- Your own past experience is your greatest asset.

> Finally, make a special effort to maintain a sense of acute observation, and recall that poetry begins with our inviting the Muse in, not necessarily waiting for her to call us. That is, poetry can be a skill as functional as journalism or fiction-writing, even if it is not possible to write a certain number of words each day.

CHAPTER 11

Telling Stories for Wholeness

Now we return to the idea of stories and their amazing power on our lives. In all experience of life, there will be stories, all put together in complex ways. What you were asked to consider earlier about narratories, and your own narratory, is important again now, as you will be asked to think about the fundamental idea of writing about yourself in a world in which stories actually define so much about identity.

The chapter will introduce the importance of the grand, large-scale stories which run parallel to your own personal experience.

Knowing stories as magic

A productive starting-point here is to reflect on the importance of stories to you when you were a child. You will have certain special moments, and perhaps even turning points in your early life in which telling stories mattered a great deal. For the writing exercises in this chapter, you need to access these stories once again and look at their nature. This is a checklist of the features of a story in the imaginative life of a child:

- The story is an escape from reality
- The story is somehow still fitted into the reality afterwards
- The story contains meanings – intended and not intended.
- The story and its power includes the listener
- The story is pretence yet returns to impact on actual experience.
- The story is an integral part of your self-knowledge

A perfect way to grasp this multi-level nature of these is to use the example of a friend telling you about an experience: notice how the teller tries to maintain interest. There are ploys we all use to do this. The friend might notice your responses and sense your boredom or your involvement, and change the pace of the story accordingly. He or she might change the nature of the language, perhaps cutting out certain words he thinks might not be acceptable to you, and so on. In other words, a story for anyone is a complex interweaving of intentions and meanings; for a child, it is simply a starting point in making personal stories.

A neat way to express this is to say that telling and listening to stories helps us to understand how all narratives

–of individuals and of nations even – are made. Even as an adult, you can continue this magic complexity, because you can tell yourself stories in your journaling. Here is an example:

Stage 1. Topic – the story of my father's autograph book.

Stage 2. Establish the subject: The autograph book was found after his death, among old postcards and letters. It was dog-eared and tatty, full of autographs of famous footballers and cricketers.

Stage 3. He was notoriously withdrawn – a shy man who would not talk about his enthusiasms; a man with no sense of joy.

Stage 4 BUT - on the inside cover of the fading old autograph book was a sketch of his school team, dated 1938. There was your father, written in as 'centre forward' and the team-sheet was in large letters and bold ink. Finally, he added, at the bottom, 'This was the team that beat Harfold Manor School 3-0 in the final...'

It is a story to relate to yourself as something formative in your understanding of others. Of course, you also add your own responses. Some possibilities might be:

Your discovery of the book and your sensations
The feeling of revelation as you se his 'other, hidden side'
The boy and the man – a contrast.

These are all possibilities for a story of the self. Now, what would be a story that would reveal an aspect of you?

> *My aim is to discover something in myself, and if I conform, I shall be failing to do this. So being an enigma energises me. I believe I am building foundations for myself.*
>
> Theodore Zeldin

Notes

For this piece of writing, think of an experience you have had which would reveal something of your essential nature. Write down the salient features of this, simply as a series of events such as finds ring/ takes it home/ thinks of the owner/ hands it to police/ gets letter later from owner/ imagined owner different from the real.

When you have written this list, develop it into a plain narrative which reveals something about your imaginative contact with the world. Add together the actual events and your own participation as a storyteller. The exercise is to look at both the story and the teller, and to relocate that magic childhood interplay between story and writer or teller.

Writing down dreams

In some journaling courses, the act of keeping a dream-diary is central to the concept of the learning process. Here it is mentioned as it provides a rich source of material about the self and self-knowledge, even if you leave out Freudian interpretation and simply make of the dream-story whatever you like. The aim is simply to write down the main features of each dream as you recall it. Of course, this is usually fragmentary. You must have experienced the retelling of a dream to someone, and feeling that sensation of the vividness receding. Sometimes the most powerful dream fades quickly into one single image and you are unable to thread it together again.

The fabric of dream-stories is the notion of a symbol and a surreal landscape, or townscape or any similar 'setting' for the dream. The imagery and its potential importance for you is the essential quality. This is a systematic way to record and develop your dreams:

1. Write a list of the main events of the dream.
2. Write or sketch the main image
3. Decide whether the 'plot' of the dream is meaningful to you.
4. If there is a central symbol, is it familiar or not?

For instance, you might dream of a tower and you are looking across a city in which there is a massive traffic-jam. You can see your partner's car in the distance, caught in the jam. You look at your watch. You feel sad. You try to wave but there is no response. You weep. The noise of the traffic increases. Then fade and wake.

In journaling, there is no need to give this a Freudian interpretation. What concerns you is simply the relation of the feelings in the dream to your current spiritual condition. You could say that it is a dream of (a) loneliness (b) distance from a partner – after a row, or (c) a sense of being removed from what your spirit desires. It may even relate to a life of noise, disorder and stress.

Your dream-diary has a great deal of potential. Consider the nature of dreams as centres of creativity:

- They ritualise and enlarge areas of life.
- They suggest an integration of dream to life
- They contain a certain type of emotional energy
- They may trigger creative work in the waking life

In the culture of the Senoi people of Malaysia, dreams are central to the understanding of life. Children talk about the night's dreaming to their parents and this is reinforced as a positive, worthwhile narrative, as the dream-life enhances and even interprets the waking life. To a writer, the dream-story is the potential centre of a whole new genesis of a state of being – of seeing yourself as if from a fresh stance, for example.

> *Before you come alive, life is nothing; it's up to you to give it meaning, and value is nothing else but the meaning that you choose.*
> Jean Paul Sartre

The usefulness in all this is to select from the dream-narrative want you see as significant. For instance, a man dreamed of eating a mountain of plum cake and eating out rooms for him to live in. Does this mean that he worries about his eating habits or that it is simply a dream of pleasure, stretched to a surreal level?

Certainly some varieties of dreams have features which are particularly useful to writers. An example would be a dream that has transformations, as when you turn into something else; or a dream that has special communications to you in words or texts or images. These are clearly worth a close inspection. It has become a common habit in some types of journaling to keep a detailed record of the categories of symbols appearing in repeated dreams. Of course, each person draws from these records a range of different reactions. The important point is that the drama in a dream is always going to be the essence: that is, the people who appear in the dream narrative, the situations and the sources of fears and so on.

It is wise to forget any established psychopathological viewpoint on your dreams. It is little use looking up Freudian symbols or Jungian archetypes, and complicating the business with unnecessary theories. What matters here is the patterns of meanings that you extract and then what you do with those meanings.

Dreams are also useful in exploiting the idea of rebellion and non-conformity. The quotation from Theodore Zeldin given above refers to how 'being an enigma energises...' A dream can hint at certain aspects of yourself which have always been a mystery. For instance, if you have ever read an interpretation of a dream in a dream dictionary, you will have noticed how easily common sense transmutes into scientific jargon: the reason is that we like mysteries. Who wants everything in life to be explained so much that it is explained away?

Do you want these inexplicable elements in yourself to be explained away? It may be that you have never actually verbalised any of this mystery. It would almost certainly pay you to log some of the unknown, often neglected aspects of your attitudes and behaviour. A plain starting-point is just to list those parts of yourself that could be seen as non-conformist. You could include:

Clothes

Political views

Taste in music

Habits of solitude

Sense of humour

The last one in the list provides an excellent example of the enigmatic ingredient in us all. Your sense of humour would be present in a dream, often in a surreal way. The cause of this might lie in your comic taste. You might enjoy and appreciate the cartoons of Gary Larson, for instance, the *Far Side* strips. These involve a grotesque counter-world to the familiar one, and a reading of them might provoke more than a simple smile at the bizarre: it is possible to read them as a critique of some aspects of the American ideology and way of life. But the chances are that you have never asked yourself why you smile and respond. Dreams often provide clues to this, and make a platform for writing.

Random responses

You can work in very specific ways with dream-stories. One productive method is to extend the events and nature of a dream by *guided imagery*. This is taking the substance of a dream and extending it into a constructed story, retaining the elements of the actual dream, and including dialogues or real events turned into fiction. Try this exercise:

1. When you have had a dream with a very vivid set of details and images, write it down quickly, noting the essential storyline.
2. Develop this into a story, just as a set of sharp events or images.
3. Stop when you feel a significant point about yourself has been reached.

Notice that you start using the techniques of crafted short stories, or sometimes the simplistic narratives of children. The real interest in this is the point you choose as the closure. It is valuable to reflect on this and ask why and how you ended as you did.

Guided imagery lends itself to a close reflection by the dreamer in the writing process. The obvious example is your need to find certain insights about current apprehensions through the narrative. Here is an example of how a dream can create a productive symbol, needing much thought in the journaling reflection:

Dream narrative:
I am an a banquet and I am surrounded by relatives, many of whom have passed away or are out of touch with me and my life. We all eat and talk but I am silent. In the middle of the dinner, something I swallow sticks in my throat – it is large and hard like a stone. I panic and try to scream for help but no-one notices. They all carry on talking as if I am not there. I run outside, terrified at the monstrous object lodged in my throat. I appeal to the faces in turn but they are all preoccupied with themselves and seem callous to me.

Response:

Simply for uses of creative writing or journaling, this dream provides plenty of material for reflection. If you leave out anything Freudian or Jungian and simply consider the possibilities of such a narrative meaning, you might have some such as these:

1. I find the family and their ideas 'hard to swallow' – I do no fit in with them.

2. I sense that the hard, individual struggle in my life is uncommunicated.
3. Pleasure – such as eating – is associated with some unpleasant thoughts (e.g. am I in the middle of a dieting programme?)

These are all examples of common sense interpretation, drawn from obvious surface meanings of the story, grotesque as it may seem in the dreaming. Consider the potential here for your creative writing, even the writing done in free flow.

A constructed storyline, extended into a short story based on your own instinctual writing, might find in this a tale of isolation, of a person alone in a crowd, making gestures but unheeded. It could be a parable of the lack of communication and understanding in the person's world. Your writing might take any one of a variety of forms:

A dialogue

A letter

A comic satire

A parable

Metanarratives: reading wider

This is a long word for a simple concept. A metanarrative is simply a larger, grander story above the story of an individual. For instance, if you look at the USA and the way the media and the film industry create images and interpretations of the 'American story' you will see common features such as the idea of the 'frontier' and the pioneers; you will have certain values built into that story, such as survival, toughness and resourcefulness. The grandeur and beauty of the land will be in the story, as will the American urban culture and the stereotypes of American people.

Every large-scale metanarrative has these kinds of elements, and of course, you fit into the picture. Have you every thought how much of your idea of your self and your own personal story relates to a metanarrative of some kind? A metanarrative could be any of these versions:

- The story of how a nation grew
- The story of an exemplary person in a given context
- Stories of a war in the formation of a people
- The reflection of a culture in pop music

This example will show how many possibilities there are in the life of one individual:

John Smith:

Version one – born at a time when Britain had an empire. Learned history from an imperial standpoint; played with toy soldiers. Wanted to be a general. Adopted male values such as bravery...

Version two – brought up in an industrial town; absorbed the virtues of hard work and self-help. Always aimed at having a 'good job' and 'settling down with a wife, children and a semi-detached house...

Think about your own possibilities as a figure who is involved in certain large-scale stories. They could be about class, race, gender, power, geography and so on. They could relate to any force which influences the way you live. Of course, these stories are inescapable, even if you lived like a recluse. But don't take this as a negative. In fact, being part of a metanarrative can be a very exciting and productive experience. You only have to consider the story of the Allied victory in world war two to see how momentous personal stories of testimony are. Or, think about the veteran soldiers who tell their part of the war in the trenches every Remembrance Day.

Of course, your own life history may parallel large, formative events in this larger story. It can also have many levels at which your experience matches the story of a country or even of an idea such as feminism or Marxism.

The interest for you and your journaling lies in how you are placed in whatever series of other stories you distinguish around you.

> *One does not become enlightened by imagining figures of light, but by making the darkness conscious.*
> Carl Jung

Of course, the enlightenment comes to each person when he or she sees their place in this larger structure. A very productive writing session should involve an exploration of your place in, say, the broader story of your regional identity. Supposing you lived in Yorkshire. Some of the narratives which would intermix to form this story of a region would be made by books; some by the mass media, some by fashion and so on. The results may well be a set of stereotypes such as the northerner with his greyhounds and pigeons and his fondness for beer.

But what about the reality of life where you are as it actually is, and as you are witness to it? A useful journaling time could be spent on affirming how you feel about yourself as a product of a time and place. You might include:

Local geography

Cultural tradition

| Language – maybe a local dialect? |

Your opinion of the metropolis

These more universal issues obviously influence your self-knowledge and your writing about this will reflect many of these issues during your growing-up.

Influences on your view of the world	Inner imaginative life
From the nation/political structures	From childhood
The world of ideas	Emotional make-up
Change in social attitudes	Change in your beliefs
Media stories of class, race, social change, place, family, work, relationships etc.	
You as a part of the larger stories of your times and contemporaries	
You as a writer	

Fig. 5   Example of a metanarrative

Metanarratives: ourselves in stories

The above illustration shows how you as a creative mind placed in the massive world-picture of great events and social change. The aspects of this to draw into your writing for yourself are the relationships of your own perception to the greater events. For instance, it would not be difficult to place yourself as a part of a national or global story of capitalism. Consider the aspects of the metanarrative of capitalism which impinge on modern urban dwellers:

- Shopping habits
- Eating at 'chain' identity restaurants
- Exposed to the same advertisements
- Given the same mass-choice items
- Offered the aspirations of capitalism – to gather wealth
- Given a profile of style and thought for your age and status

A fascinating way to develop writing about yourself here is to expand on the way you differ from the 'average' person envisaged by those powerful people who set the style and tone of modern life in a capitalist framework.

Reflections

Write about your individuality now, with the discussion of metanarratives in mind. For instance, start by listing your lifestyle habits which are in opposition to anything you consider to be your expected behaviour. Examples might be:

Shopping at small business/craft shops, not chains

Cooking at home – not eating microwave meals or convenience foods

Drinking an unfashionable drink

Reading books by obscure writers- never mentioned in newspaper reviews.

Now write about your individual sense of self, concentrating on a pen-portrait of yourself as if you were writing a column for a magazine. You could use the structure of 1. Basic attitudes to modern life 2. Use of technology 3. Attitudes to fashionable things 4. Your expression of personal taste etc.

Parables for understanding

You will be familiar with the form of a parable from the bible, as in the story of the Prodigal Son. Stories told with a definite meaning or interpretation provide us with the next significant step towards the self-understanding in your writing journal. The aim here is now to frame your self and life in this larger context by writing about yourself as a figure in a modern parable. Here is an example:

He was a man who had lived in a quiet country backwater, but who dreamed of becoming a famous film-director. As a boy, he had drawn cartoons and images in notebooks, then later taken a deep interest in cameras. Every day he would imagine innovative shots made by a camera, and all life was a subject for him. He thought up storylines that could be told in pictures. He even drew storyboards based on dramatic stories he read in newspapers.

> *But he left the village to go to a massive city and learn the art at a university. There, everything turned sour. No-one said he was any good at filming. His ideas had all been said before. There seemed nothing new to say or show. He changed courses and studied business and economics. People said that banking was an excellent career.*

But today, ten years on, he still makes a square with his hands and imagines a camera-shot. It's a joke in the office, and he laughs with his colleagues. But in his room he still has his first camera and a file of photographs, scripts and cuttings.

Notice how this depicts a very typical story – not only the 'big fish in a little pond' idea but also the artist who betrays his vocation, the 'selling out' story. So what would be your own parable? Whatever it is, you need to bear in mind these aspects of parables (sometimes the word allegory might be used):

- Talking about a surface event but with a hidden reference
- Having a strong moral or philosophical purpose
- Simple, elemental stories
- Universal appeal across cultures
- They reveal the essentials, missing out details and sub-plots etc.

Some potentially interesting themes for parables are the basic, universal ones such as betrayal, guilt, the challenge, the quest, failure, innocence and love. In your preparation, read some of the popular ones, such as parables about common perceptions, as in the story of the three men who pass the carcass of a dead dog on the road. The first men says, 'Ugh! What an awful smell from that dog!' The second man looks and says, 'Ah, the wretched thing looks foul, decomposing..' But the third man sees something different and says, simply: 'That dog has beautiful eyes.'

After all, parables are the oldest stories, and were often part of an oral tradition. Notice how a writer is able to draw on a range of basic symbols in this exercise. The central image in a parable – what the language implies – is the key to the story. For instance, you might take the idea of stone and its qualities, and build a parable around that.

STONE

It suggests lack of feeling, no responses, endures all 'weathers' etc.

No particular shape or form.

But can be sculptured

Once you reach that third point and realise that you have the kernel of a story, you are close to making a successful and powerful piece of writing. The reason for this is that you can make a narrative from the idea that a stone becomes a shape with a meaning – or the person in your story turns from something without shape or being into a person with meaning.

Writing in trauma

One of the most profound aspects of writing in regard to extreme pain and suffering is in the case of coping with death. Of course, some of the greatest literature in he language is concerned with death and bereavement, but everyone knows the stressful situation of being unable to talk about anything significant in the face of such loss. This is where the distancing of writing as if in parables plays a useful part.

This enables us to write from a less involved point of view. When bereavement seems to numb all the senses and prevents normal communication, the written word comes into its own. This is why a great poem such as Tennyson's *In Memoriam* is so remarkable. It is a lament for the loss of a dear friend by a young man, a fellow student at Cambridge, and the poem also questions God" purpose and searches for the meaning, if any in a young person's death.

The point is that Tennyson's poem suggests a profitable way to express those difficult thoughts at such a painful time. You can re-tell the life as if from an objective standpoint, and recreate significant moments in that life. This is very similar to the way we speak of the dead with fondness when recalling funny events or loving moments with them. This kind of writing, as if telling a simple but universal story about an individual, is illustrated in Thomas Hardy's poem, *Afterwards,* in which he imagines the way people will speak about him after his death:

> If it be in the dusk when, like an eyelid's soundless blink,
>> The dew-fall hawk comes crossing the shades to alight
>> Upon the wind-warped upland thorn, a gazer may think,
>> "To him, this must have been a familiar sight."

Hardy's intonation and attitude to the lived life and the end of one individual life provides us with a template for writing at moments of personal trauma. The idea is to assemble a series of impressions of the dead person and then telling yourself their story –a testament to a process of loving and living. You might list these aspects like this:

She used to walk the garden at seven each day
She fed all animals – even strays
Her learning to paint ruined the lounge carpet
Her whistling was always irritating

Notice how this gives a set intonation pattern, like the undervoice discussed in the chapter on poetry. In fact, the idea extends into any writing about loss or separation, or for any point in life at which you wish to bring someone to mind. It may even be a memory of a valuable friendship now ceased.

Parables, then, provide a distancing process; this makes the subjects at several removes from the often uncomfortable closeness which makes understanding and reflection difficult to achieve.

Case Study

Lesley was someone who had always taken an interest in politics. She even did a course in modern government and began to participate in local politics. At work, she was always one of the leading representatives in the trade union, and she developed a profound understanding of how power works and how individuals function in power systems. Corporate identity was a phrase that made her reach for the rule book.

But she became frustrated at the apathy shown by her colleagues. They all seemed to complain about things such as the union journal was concerned with labour exploitation in the Third World but did nothing for their own working conditions. The whole business became frustrating for her, and yet she had so much to say. She had the habit of internalising her thoughts, and letting things rankle inside, never finding an outlet for their expression.

It was when she noticed a man on the tube going to work writing in a notebook that she realised how helpful that would be. The man was clearly noting points down in preparation for a business meeting; but Lesley thought of a better use. She knew that it was a simple solution for her.

When Lesley saw that keeping a few notes about the political issues involved in all this, she began to see that simply writing down the muddle around her helped her to find insights into not only the crowd's behaviour, but her own angle on things. None of this changed the attitudes of the employees, but it changed her own conception of politics, as it forced her to express the relation of self to organisation so necessary in her work. What the journaling did for her was provide a basis for questioning her own stance on the power she saw, and on why she had become so motivated.

In fact, the habit had the added bonus of forcing her to shape and direct her thoughts. She actually produced meditations and reflection which worked neatly into small but concise essays on specific aspects of power and responsibility. It even made her a better speaker.

Summary

In this chapter you have been asked to expand your reflections and questions into the realm of world-scale stories of power, politics and social change. The skills of self-reflection in your notebook stemming from this knowledge have provided you with some fresh approaches to writing about your own perceptions. These skills and techniques are:

- Keeping a dream-diary as part of the journal
- Working with the metanarrative in contrast to your own stories
- Constructing stories for yourself for understanding
- Using parables as ways of looking with new perceptions of your life

CHAPTER 12

Bringing Writing into the Centre

Everything you have been asked to do in this book stems from the central belief that every form of personal writing has some kind of beneficial effect on the individual. Recent research has shown that even a simple diary-keeping habit is a healing process. James Pennebaker of the University of Texas puts stress on the act of 'disclosure' as something we need for mental health. But this book has aimed to reach wider and deeper. Whether or not you wish to take your creative writing further and take your writing into the public domain, you have been well prepared for this, or simply for continuing with your journaling as a monitor on your self-development.

This final chapter is aimed at giving you the option of taking your writing further if you wish to do so.

Summary of progress: keeping subject files

You may not realise this, but your habits of preparing for writing and then going though your small rituals towards quite substantial reflection and imaginative discourse have prepared you for almost any variety of writing. If you wish to enlarge on this, and concentrate on exploring some of your subjects more exhaustively, you might consider how to develop this. One way is to start a process of splitting your subjects into discrete areas. For instance, a freelance writer will usually keep and update subject files on their area of expertise. This gives you a developing resource centre to use whether or not you intend to write for others. A typical working method would be like this:

Example:

Subjects of interest

Parents and children/ local history/ religious belief/ lives of immigrants/ changing landscapes

Development

Notice how these may have grown quite naturally from your interests in your own family history, and the stories you have made of them. Your narratory or metanarrative, for example, may have expanded from how your parents met to a story of immigration. This can be developed into public writing by researching the wider subject.

Monitoring information

In an index file or a loose-leaf file with transparent pockets, label files alphabetically and arrange your subjects to a personally significant system. Each topic will split into subsidiary ones like this:

Immigration

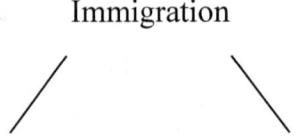

Being a stranger - political factors - occupations - social life

Random responses

With this method in mind, you can explore one example of your subjects from earlier in this book. For instance, if you choose one aspect of your own past which is now seen in a different light after being written about, take the subject and brainstorm as many aspects of it as possible in five minutes. Then rank these in order of how much you actually know about it. You might take ten aspects of your childhood, then rank them according to how much detail you recall about certain things.

Take the top three or four aspects and examine them in terms of how you can split them into separate areas. This usually causes new perspectives to emerge. You can them write about these, in a few notes, and start to enlarge them into subjects for your files. Photographs are valuable resources in this.

> *In the having mode we are bound to what we have amassed in the past: money, land, fame, social status, knowledge, children, memories. We think about the past, and we feel by remembering feelings...We are the past; we can say: 'I am what I was.'*
>
> Erich Fromm: To Have or to Be?

Sharing it all: starting a read-write group

Part of the pleasure of writing a new life for yourself is that writing things down starts a process of revelation: a gradual realisation of what relationships and friendships are really about. In the act of writing about significant others in your life, you will have inevitably had to look again at friendship and at what people mean or have meant to you. Although writing is a lonely business, there is no reason why both your writing and the wellspring of your creativity —your reading – cannot be linked to others.

There has been a recent mushrooming of reading groups, often linked to local libraries. In terms of writing, there is also a well-established tradition of support-groups for writing, but why not bring the two together and start a read-write group?

This is a group of writers eager to share their thoughts and themes, yet not particularly think about trying to be published. The sharing of reading experienced may be mixed with writing on a related subject. The advantages are clear:

- Feedback of writing is given
- Objective views of your writing are obtained
- The meetings are purely social and very productive
- There need not be a structure –simply a theme
- It facilitates the transition from private to public writing

In other words, it is a way of sliding neatly from self-reflection into meeting your first readership and response. A useful method of holding this together is to have a theme, as if you were editing an anthology. For instance:

Thematic read-write session
1. The group chooses a theme that interests all: it might be simply 'parents'
2. The next session everyone brings two pieces of writing – one in print and one of their own.
3. The group has a 'read-around'
4. Related topics are discovered and compared. It may be, for instance, that three people have all written about the influence of grandparents on their own parents.

This is the basis of a kind of group anthology. But more important, it provides your first insight into the valuable exercise of discussing responses. Notice that, until this last chapter, you have stood back from your own imaginative writing and judged yourself, often as if you were a stranger. Now you can compare this with others' responses to what you produce.

A bonus from this is that you are given more material for your personal writing. Most writers enjoy this process as it spurs them on to more ambitious work, or even more innovative writing.

Reflections

The preceding example of a read-write group is based on the assumption that your journaling has reached a peak, and that there is a need to open out into public writing. Why would such a development be necessary for some? There are several well-established reasons:

1. All creative work ultimately seeks to communicate and to share
2. Your imagination has a value beyond your own needs and uses.
3. Everyone needs feedback – for justification more than judgement

This is a simple writing exercise for your journal which illustrates this move into public writing. Take a common, universal theme such as the humour of misunderstanding. Write two passages, one exactly recounting a personal experience and a second which embellishes the experience for a short story opening. For example:

Passage one: personal reflection
The Mistake
I was once asked to assemble a desk for my son's room. I bought a kit, then started work in the spare bedroom, following the instructions carefully. It took four hours and tried my patience at times. But eventually there it was – finished and ready to use. I simply had to move the desk into the room.

It was too large to be carried through the door! After a long time thinking what to do, I asked for some help to carry it through a window, then across the landing into his room. It just fitted in.

Passage two: for another reader
I knew that my tendency to rush in and work quickly would be my undoing. The fiasco of the desk shows me at my worst in this. I had to assemble the desk for my son, and I worked steadily for hours, not stopping to think how the

dimensions of the finished product might be a problem, as I was working in a large spare room. The problem emerged as I looked at the finished desk with momentary satisfaction.

The door of the room was very narrow. The desk would never fit through there!

Notice how the second passage is assembled by craft, by a certain artificial framing of the authentic language, to add a purpose and to aim more directly at an imagined reader.

Health and wealth in your writing

You may not be aware of it, but the last few chapters of this book have also concerned the idea that writing is in itself a valuable 'therapy' for any sense of displacement or lack of purpose in life. People often comment, after writing workshops, that simply by having an invisible 'listener' in the page of the journal, they acquire the sense of release often found in confiding in someone about a problem. Even with a reader in mind, which you may now be considering, the act of writing is itself a kind of treatment, a reparation for damage done in the combats of life. Writing has some fundamental qualities which should have emerged for you in following the workshop of one idea:

- It involves a physical effort, and so your 'exercise' is felt
- There are tangible rewards and a product
- It preserves against time and change
- It encourages the therapy of meditation
- Writing is 'outside time': you are so engrossed in the action and mental patterning that time is eclipsed (awareness of time)

These may be obvious to some, but if you have not yet introduced a ritual element, then be reminded now of some simple techniques which all enhance the physical and mental effort involved:

Place: Any stable, flat surface in a quiet room

Time: Any time which invites quietude

Mood: Write to the mood that dominates and use the mood in words.

Objects: Crucially important – use objects with personal significance.

An example – photograph and meditation

Keep a board in front of you in the place where you write, and add photographic images and cuttings on this. At each session, choose an image and meditate on it, following these questions:

1. What would the sounds and smells have been?
2. What is that person thinking?
3. What might have been the unspoken thoughts on that occasion?
4. Colours and shapes – which are the significant ones there?

The writing process is part of a healthy discipline, providing your mind with an ongoing set of challenges, moving from what is known already to a less comfortable test of capacity and skill. The wealth lies in the richness of what your imagination will possess after time has elapsed. By this, it is generally felt that a treasure of experience is only worthwhile when determinedly monitored and even given a certain shape. But it is adversity that teaches.

Your writing so far will inevitably have dealt with the obstacles in life you have overcome, and the words you use will demonstrate the value of the practice. Examples are numerous, but here is one, based on a student who wrote a journal as part of a recovery programme from a drug-abuse problem:

Stage one:
Shock and adaptation to a new 'self' and environment
Explaining the fear through humour

Stage two:

Language used to define the new experience. Through words, understanding was reached.

Stage three:

Challenge – a record of how survival and the possibility of success were maintained through new friendships.

Stage four:

The writing (now several thousand words) *became an identity in itself, a separate condition.*

This last point is very important for you at your final stage now. Notice how the sheer body of language you have accrued is discretely different from you. You will re-read things you wrote six weeks ago and not recognise the person reflected there, nor even recall the experience that prompted the writing. You have attained that state of healthy distance from which more accurate and unbiased judgements of yourself may be made. But the journal has become 'distant' in these ways:

- It contains fragments integral to a former state of being
- The language may not seem to be 'yours'
- It has a quality of *becoming, not being.*
- Its language may be far-removed from your everyday words

♦ Strangely, the words impact on the present – and you never expected that!

These thoughts all give rise to the conclusion that writing in order to develop yourself is in fact about a need for change and revision that is only recognised in the doing. Therefore, your sense of the writer in you at an earlier period being different, or even *alien* to you now, is a healthy sign. Healthy because it has enabled you to revise with understanding, placing your emergent self in the frame of passing time.

Research has shown that 'the pen is mightier than the pill' in some ways. An experiment done at the University of Dakota involving asthma and arthritis sufferers asked to keep journals, had results which suggested clinical improvement in their symptoms of over 50%, compared to an improvement of only 24% in the control group. (see *The Guardian* 13.4.99)

Of course, 'turning off' the controlling function of your mind also adds a creative perspective. There is a part of the brain that operates through the randomness and 'dream-state' nature of writing, and this is good for you, as it removes the focus of stress and anxiety in the normal functioning of life. This is why free-flow writing is recommended as a regular habit in your journal. Some writers begin each session with five minutes of free flow and avoid any conscious direction towards writing about a given subject.

Applying the skills –beyond your journal

Of course, you need not involve other people directly. If you feel the need to extend your writing into social commentary, or even to entertain or address questions of identity common to all, then there are various options open to you. But the first question is, why extend your writing into open, public communication? The most common answer is perhaps to be found in the need to share, and the urge in writing to find something empathic. In short, writing justifies a life. It is a kind of valid testimony to how one specific life was experienced and 'used'. The parable of using your talents is relevant here. If you have been consistently writing your journal up to this point, then you will automatically find that you have been starting to deal with universal questions of being and self-knowledge.

What possibilities are open to you if you wish to take these skills further, and into print? You could try any one of these options:

- ♦ Joining a writer's circle

- Studying readership and audience – writing for a prescribed reader
- Focusing on one category or genre of writing
- Submitting writing for a magazine or anthology
- Learning more in a correspondence course/ Open College course

It would be helpful for you to know what aspects of your writing to date would be suited to some of these. Basically, the basis of what you have written is autobiographical. You have been assembling a portfolio of life-writing (without realising this of course). The next step is quite simple: look for the range of options for life-writing, either in fact or in fiction. Remember that a great deal of fiction is autobiographical anyway.

Notes

A useful and insightful way to try this out is just to write notes on some passages of autobiography you come across in magazines or books currently available. Research the popular autobiographies and pinpoint exactly how they have located similar areas of life-experience to your own journaling. Many classic autobiographies have succeeded simply because of the honesty of the attitudes to the life-experienced depicted.

Example:

You could look at a successful piece of writing such as *Angela's Ashes* by Frank McCourt (1997). Notice here that the writer brings together three areas of influence on ordinary lives: the Catholic church, poverty and the geography of lives caught within time and place. The interest he creates through describing poverty and disease is the obvious example: any writer could take the same basic stuff of time past and bring out the human significance. Your writing about your past has been the same essence as Frank McCourt's: now learn exactly how he makes his testimony special and significant. One answer is the confrontation with hard truth, of course. You might take one important experience like this example, and ask these questions:

- Why did that happen?
- Was I influential on the event?
- What did I learn?
- What did I not learn?

Brainstorming in the final workshop

Your last workshop is totally concerned with your own vision of your new life. After all, much of this book has been based on the human tendency to concentrate on goals and aspirations, rather than note in the present exactly what aims were fulfilled. In other words, this session takes you back to the 'tour of the house' game in which you looked at all the blessings you have in ordinariness.

But this time, you are to revisit a series of stages which led to the person you are now. Here is the exercise:

1. Think about these three points in your recent past –
One year ago
Two years ago
Five years ago
2. For each one, write down the important, influential elements in your life at the time. This could be people, jobs, events etc.
3. Now extract the learning that was taking place at each stage. This might be – five years ago/ learning to drive. Two years ago/ first computer and learning e-mail and so on.
4. From the three stages, list all the things you have learned in that five-year period. It may be something as

simple as how to change a nappy or change a wheel on a car!

5. Finally, set similar stages for the five years ahead, and write what learning you expect to achieve at the three stages.

What you have here is a neat comparison of past and future, to set beside the career-focussed goals so often thrust upon us. For example, if you have just graduated from college, the normal goals will probably be to acquire 'transferable skills' as soon as possible. Such things as driving, being computer-literate, writing a c.v. and similar skills. The problem with this is that it masks the achievements brought about by the inevitable changes involved in that study towards graduation. These might range from negotiating with landlords to planning a budget.

In other words, this final workshop is about the invisible goals. These are the ones we take for granted. So write about any such achievements you have made, and explain to yourself the nature of those achievements. You might even set it out like a report.

Another variant of this if you prefer is to sketch a 'storyboard of the significant stages of your life. If you were asked to sketch ten scenes which you now see as crucially important in forming the person you are now, what people, places and words would be central to those storyboard 'shots'? Imagine a cartoon-strip with the usual skipping of unnecessary detail, and cuts to the next scene: what would be the essentials in your case?

Narratories into everyday life

Let us recap the importance of the narratory for this course. Remember that this is your imposed bundle of stories: the stories which form you as a social being, composed by others. It is the tale told about you multiplied by the number of tellers. In taking this principle further, the notion of writing your own narratory is fundamental to the 'new life' the journaling here has offered you. Research has shown that the 'feel good' factor from this writing is no delusion. Dr. Geoffrey Lowe at the University of Hull has said the basis of this good mental health is something to do with the association between psychological unwinding and our immune system. (see further reading).

In short, make this disclosure in self-writing a part of your routine and you will decrease the possibility of stress being a factor in your working life. The creativity inherent in this ritual and meditation is an added bonus, but it is integral to the whole process. You can take the usefulness of the narratory further by increasing your use of these devices in your journaling:

- Projecting your story into the future
- Imagining a child's eye view of yourself
- Telling the story of your failures as a kind of success
- Inventing words to explain yourself –rejecting existing words
- Avoiding all words which give a value-judgement

The important point is that the writing must always be a ritual. You are re-telling what has been already known, but not properly understood, and even sometimes taken for granted. Your own set of narratories is never complete, and you are always, at every stage of life, in the middle of another which is being generated. Your journal is therefore a mirror of that developing story, telling about you again, in yet another version. For these reasons, the potential for re-telling is made of infinite options and versions.

The strongest narratory will always be the parable, as this simplifies your story, in order to provide a story to 'decode' and to take to pieces in order to find new insights previously hidden by familiarity. The difficult part is in isolating the things that happen to you and framing them in terms of understanding their working within the broader frame of society and history.

Example of one storyline in a narratory

For instance, you might take one aspect of your work routine and write about it with a historical perspective, like this:

Grandfather – sense of time – clocking in at work. Strict hours. Job involved paper rather than computer memory.

Father – Similar, but began using technology to a small extent – calculating machine and electronic typewriter.

You – similar work, in an office, but very little paper filing! Flexitime and e-mail – concepts totally alien to previous generations.

Significance of this?
Conception of time
Notion of work as a quantifiable product
Specialism more acute

Your writing response might be to access the working lives of your family in the past, through talking to living relatives and studying photographic records. Local archives related to particular industries often provide unusual stimulus material for writing about work.

A common approach to this kind of material is to write an account of your working day, perhaps in documentary style, than imagine a day in the life of a grandparent at work. This provides an imaginative perspective on your own job and its rewards as well as its demands. For instance, some occupations in the tanning industry used to require workers to spend seven hours a day bent over a large barrel, cleaning skins. Trying to imagine the mind of a worker in such conditions is obvious extremely difficult, but your own daily work, however familiar to you, will be strange to others who have never been close to that work: not as extreme as the tanning example, but known intimately and 'from the inside' by yourself.

Summary

This chapter has brought together some of the strands of this concept of journaling. A final summary of the nature of this course is contained in these points:

- The basis of the writing is total honesty about yourself
- The recognition of your past as being formative of your present
- Techniques of creative writing can be tranferred for use

- Your imagination is limitless and has truths in itself
- Your real story is not contained in your narratories
- Standing back from the everyday is essential

The core of the whole set of activities is in the confrontation with the possibilities inherent in your present and past imaginative life. This is why your own ritual is so important. You should have made the writing rituals central to all your writing sessions now. As was noted earlier in this chapter, the rituals will come, quite naturally, in the use of time: people tend to do things with stages and structure rather than in one uniform action.

Naturally, the exercises have been about affirmation. You should have found that at least some of your writing pieces will have opened out significant insights for you – sometimes notable revelations. Mystics and poets often talk about those moments of incredible insight into the meaning of life: what Wordsworth called being 'Surprised by joy' and what the critic Marghanita Laski spoke of as 'ordinary ecstasy': the moments when you sense an understanding of time and life. These are not rare in life-writing of any kind. But in your case, maybe you would like to log the nature of the most astonishing writing you have done throughout the book. Categories might be:

1. A moment of sheer joy in living
2. A sense of being thankful
3. Feeling happy even in adversity
4. A desire to communicate and share a specific insight
5. A feeling of paradox, of contradiction, which is resolved in the writing.

The course is also a basis for truthful meditation on the focal influences on what has made you the person you are now. If you have followed the exercises meticulously, you should now be on a vantage-point from which your overview of the journey of your life should be visible. At the heart of the book is the assumption that the act of writing is an empowerment. It enables you to see through the crowding and clamour of modern life to study the person who is yourself, even in the middle of that pace and haste towards worldly success.

Your own version of success is a close contact with your honestly expressed self: a being always emerging, growing and learning. Writing is the simplest and most powerful way to access that self at each stage of growth.

If you wish to go further and be a writer with an audience, always keep close to that process of discovery and self-discovery brought about by the methods of disclosure you have adopted here. But the main purpose has been to provide you with a set of stimuli to further exploration of those 'alternative' versions of yourself which were discussed in the first chapter. Remember that we are all complex and unknown, ultimately, beneath the social veneer. Yet what could be more disenchanting than to let the colour and relish in life pass by simply because no effort to recall and reflect on things was ever done.

Writing of any kind will always assert belief and express reasons for life being both perplexing yet universally experienced as a set of human values adapted to cultures and states of mind. At the common heart of the diversity is language: the distinguishing ability of *homo sapiens*. In oral cultures – those with no written system and alphabet, poets recall important events by using memory-devices and they embellish the basic facts with formulas of words. In our advanced literate cultures in Europe and America for instance, the advancement of language often appears to clutter the sharpness of experience, to mask the reality in cumbersome words and abstraction.

Writing for your new life is a move towards recapturing some of that spontaneity and verve in the oral cultures – to let your own words speak through the schoolroom and the mass of information thrown at you every day. In this fundamental respect, writing is always an act of defiance against all the negative forces, reminding you of what is valuable in your life.

Now that you have acquired these writing habits, go forward with these guidelines in mind:

- Treat your writing as naturally as you do your cleaning or dressing
- Never leave out any words because of moral choice –go for truth!
- Try not to over-intellectualise the material
- Always try to stand back from experience
- Start by describing and move on to reflection
- Remember that your life is unique – so include 'ordinariness'

Writing has made new lives: there is a vast library of autobiographies to prove it. Several examples could be given of people who, even very late in life, decided to put their words before their unregistered mass of life-experience and found renewal.

A Last Affirmative Statement

Everything I have written above is one mentor's angle on language and change- personal change. There is an assumption in the media that change in self-development is bound to be good. Of course, it is not so, and consequently, each self knows, by good feeling and a sense of achievement and satisfaction, that a change has been beneficial. I am trusting in my advice and guidance in this book because the approach has helped me. All I can do is pass on that affirmation that writing joy, based on truth, will give you every chance of success in the aim of achieving the best kind of change.

Further Reading and Reference

Books

Carole Blake, *From Pitch to Publication* (Macmillan, 1999)
Gillie Bolton, *The Therapeutic Potential of Creative Writing* (Kingsley, 1999)
Erich Fromm, *To Have or To Be?* (Cape, 1978)
Natalie Goldberg, *Writing Down the Bones* (Shambhala, 1986)
Nicki Jackowska, *Write for Life* (Element, 1997)
Ursula K. Le Guin, *Steering the Craft* (Eighth Mountain Press, 1998)
G.Lynn Nelson, *Writing and Being* (Luramedia, 1994)
Tristine Rainer, *The New Diary* (Penguin Putnam, 1978)
Fiona Sampson, *The Healing Word* : a practical guide to poetry and personal development activities) (Poetry Society 2000)
Myra Schneider & John Killick, *Writing for Self-Discovery* (Element, 1998)
Susan Sellers (ed.) *Taking Reality by Surprise* (Women's Press, 1994)
John Singleton and Mary Luckhurst, ed. The Creative Writing Handbook (Macmillan, 2000)
Michael C.Smith & Suzanne Greenberg, *Everyday Creative Writing* (NTC, 1996)
Anthony Storr, *Solitude* (HarperCollins,1997)
P.E. Vernon, *Creativity* (Penguin, 1982)
John Whale, *Put it in Writing* (Orion, 1999)

Journals and magazines on writing

For*ewords,* Park Terrace Courtyard, Park Terrace East, Horsham, West Sussex RH13 5DJ

Mslexia   PO box 656, Newcastle upon Tyne, NE99 2XD (Available only by subscription)
The New Writer, PO box 60, Cranbrook, Kent TN17 2 ZR
Writing Magazine, PO box 168, Wellington Street, Leeds, LS1 1RF
Writers' Forum, PO box 3229, Bournemouth BH1 1ZS

Note: There is also a great deal of relevant information on research done in this area in various magazines such as *Here's Health* and *Zest*. These often combine case studies with accounts of recent research done on using creative writing as part of self-development.

The magazine of the National Association of Writers in Education, *Writing in Education,* also has a great deal of relevant information, and they also have a website. Details are:
NAWE, PO Box 1, Sheriff Hutton, York YO60 7YU
www.nawe.co.uk
The netsite of NAWE leads you to a whole range of sites from organisations with an interest in writing and personal development. This includes the latest (April, 2000) called The Reading Room which has every aspect of creative writing: www.reading-room.org.uk

Organisations

If you would like to take this subject further, are you might be interested in courses, groups and activities associated with either writing and therapy or writing and personal development, then these organisations are useful:
The Arvon Foundation, Totleigh Barton, Sheepwash, Beaworthy, Devon EX21 5NS
Arvon have many taught short courses, but they also arrange *writers' retreats,* at which you spend a week with other people

who write or are starting to write, and simply have time to be creative.

Healing Arts, St. Mary's, Parkhurst Road, Newport, Isle of Wight PO30 5TG

Health and the Arts Director: Terry Smyth, Colchester Institute, Sheepen Road, Colchester, Essex CO3 3LL

LAPIDUS   - The Association for the Literary Arts in Personal Development, has been established since 1996. Details from: The Administrator, LAPIDUS, Coben Associates, 2nd floor, 3, The Plain, Thornbury, Bristol BS35 2 AG   Website: www.lapidus.org.uk

The Poetry Society, 22, Betterton Street, London, WC2H 9BU
(They have just published a handbook on writing and health-see above list)

Sheffield Writing Development Project, Eventus, The Workstation, 15, Paternoster Row, Sheffield S1 2BX

This project is very active in organising events around writing and self-development. In April, 2000, they held a major conference, with celebrated speakers such as Dannie Abse, and accounts of on-going research on topics such as 'Writer in the surgery'

Survivors Poetry, Diorama Arts centre, 34 Osnabrook Street, London NW1 3ND

University of Sussex : on offer is a Diploma in Creative Writing and Personal Development (one year).

Chat Rooms and Writing Magazines on the Net

Another interesting development in this area has been the arrival of writing 'loops' for interchange of information and anthologies of writing. A basic one, leading to others, is Anointed by Daemons at http://homepage.dtn.ntl.com

Basically, your best source of updated information for all varieties of writing activities, including journaling, readers' groups and support groups, is your regional arts organisation. The Yorkshire Arts newsletter, *Writeangles,* for instance, provides information on courses, groups, anthologies, submissions and sources of advice.

Other interesting and useful developments are the writing magazines: some of them are dedicated to particular categories and genres, but many are looking for original imaginative writing and also have a great deal on writing and personal development or writing as therapy. Typical examples are:
blocwriters@hatmail.com
hackwriters.com

Proof   www.shu.ac.uk/proof/proof.htm
Trace   http://trace.ntu.ac.uk

There is a mass of information about publications for writers, groups and societies, in Barry Turner's annual *The Writer's Handbook* (Macmillan) and in the annual *Writers' and Artists' Yearbook* (A & C Black). This publication also lists universities and specialist organisations which offer summer courses in writing.

Academic research on writing and health

These references are made in the book:
Hilary Bower   *The Guardian* April 13 1999:
Th*e Pen is Mightier than the Pill:* This is an excellent summary of relevant research, including work done in the USA and by Dr. Geoffrey Lowe at the University of Hull.
Rita Carter in *The New Scientist* (8 Oct. 1999) in *Tune in, Tune Off* pp.30-34, discusses research into creativity and the brain.
Joyce Carol Oates, in *The Guardian* July 22 1999 provides a useful insight into physical exercise and writing, linking her running regime to the kind of meditation provided in journaling.

www.ingramcontent.com/pod-product-compliance
Lightning Source LLC
LaVergne TN
LVHW051826080426
835512LV00018B/2737